BHU

BHU

From Inception to Crisis (1915–65)

Saumya Dey

ink | OCCAM

ISBN: 978-93-6547-218-9

First published in India 2025
This edition published 2025

BluOne Ink Pvt. Ltd
A-76, 2nd Floor, Sector 136, Noida
Uttar Pradesh 201301
www.bluone.ink
publisher@bluone.ink

Printed and bound in India By Thomson Press Indi Ltd.

Kali and Occam are imprints of BluOne Ink

|| ॐ नमो भगवते रुद्राय ||

अतुलितबलधामं हेमशैलाभदेहं, अनुजवनकृशानुं ज्ञानिनामग्रगण्यम्।
सकलगुणनिधानं वानराणामधीशं, रघुपतिप्रियभक्तं वातजातं नमामि।

To Rishihood University, with affection and gratitude

Contents

Acknowledgements

I owe my sincerest thanks and gratitude to my institution, Rishihood University. I could not have undertaken and completed this book project without its ever-present support. I am also grateful to the staff at the Pradhan Mantri Museum and Library (PMML), where I conducted the bulk of my research, for their kind assistance and cooperation.

Introduction

The Birth of the Modern World, 1780–1914[1] is a voluminous monograph authored by the late British historian C.A. Bayly (1945–2015, he taught at the University of Cambridge). As the title indicates, the book seeks to document the emergence of what we commonly refer to as 'modernity' in general parlance in its various aspects. Interestingly, as we observe, the process, in Bayly's understanding, was enabled or underpinned by colonialism. For instance, global mercantilist networks of exchange, industrialization-driven urbanism, the Western-style centralized bureaucratic state and organized religion, liberalism, and Western aesthetic values are some seminal frameworks of modernity identified by him. The world, Bayly implicitly argues, became 'modern' as Western countries forcefully brought the non-Western societies into their ambit through colonial domination and irrevocably transformed them. In other words, one might say, he seems to interpret modernity as the global spread of some Western-origin paradigms and outlooks with the colonized Asian and African 'natives' partaking in and adopting them.

The most glaring deficiency in Bayly's schema is its excessive simplicity. It is undeniable that colonialism transformed the non-Western societies in multiple ways by bringing to them certain Western-derived economic and political frameworks and social, cultural, and intellectual influences. Nevertheless, unlike what Bayly seems to suggest, non-Western societies were not always passive recipients of everything that came their way through the route of colonialism. In the Indian context, for instance, British colonial domination triggered a massive intellectual churn within native society. As we observe, many Indian elites critically engaged with the transferences from the metropole and demonstrated the capacity to come up with fairly original intellectual positions as well as social and cultural initiatives. To give an example, their reaction to Christianity, the colonizers' creed, was not one of abject surrender. They did not simply abandon their ancestral religions and convert wholesale. Instead, they responded to the Christian proselytizers' criticisms of their religious practices and social order by initiating various reforms therein. Rabindranath Tagore (1861–1941) eloquently critiqued the Western-style centralized bureaucratic state and the 'nationalism' it articulated,[2] while Mohandas Karamchand Gandhi (1869–1948) rejected the industrial capitalist framework of economic production and the urban life it fostered.[3] Apparently, the latter could do so because, to a significant extent, peasant and artisanal production was still intact in his country. Gandhi's social and economic philosophy, therefore, drew inspiration from what he saw to be a viable alternative to Western civilization. Although India had been integrated into an economic 'world system' by Great Britain as a periphery, its traditional, autarkic rural economy did not cease to exist. Even the urbanism that took shape in the industrial centres (and other parts) of colonial India was by no means a completely unique social formation; it was replete with traditional social practices and mores.

Moving on to art, first Raja Ravi Varma (1848–1906) and then the 'Bengal school' of painters[4] (at Visva-Bharati University in Shantiniketan) did adopt the Western academic style, but they also lent it a distinctly Indian appearance. Again, from Ram Mohun Roy (1772–1833) to Madan Mohan Malaviya (1865–1946), Indians demonstrated the capacity to adopt Western liberal values and yet remain steadfast in their own cultural and religious convictions.

What eventually emerged as modernity in India was not a mere replication of phenomena derived from Great Britain. The formation of Indian modernity was an ambiguous and dialogic process. It certainly comprised adoptions from the metropole and the Western world at large, but these adoptions were generally transformed and considerably Indianized by the conscious, critical agency of Indian elites or the unconscious weight of tradition as represented by the vast Indian masses. This book is primarily an account of the first five decades of one of the foremost Indian universities. This brief history may also, to a considerable extent, be read as an episode in the formation of the dialogic Indian modernity.

Rather curiously, *The Birth of the Modern World* does not allude to the way colonialism assaulted the traditional epistemes of native societies by exposing them to frameworks of Western knowledge. The marginalization of traditional learning, amounting to its near erasure, is arguably the most unmistakable way in which Asian and African societies were transformed by colonialism. In India, for instance, as depicted in Chapter 1, traditional schools and the education imparted therein were nearly extinct parallel to the establishment and expansion of British colonial administration. They were, as we shall see, neglected into oblivion by the white rulers of the country. In due course, the classical learning cultivated by the social elites, pertaining to jurisprudence and literature, fared no better, despite being initially patronized by the colonial administration.

As the British started to acquire political mastery of India, they initiated a multifaceted knowledge-gathering exercise about it. Focused on understanding the country better (so that they ruled it efficiently), their cognitive framework at this stage was chiefly 'Orientalist'. What is meant by this is that it generally centred around textual studies in the classical eastern (or 'Oriental') languages such as Sanskrit, Persian, and Arabic. The officials of the East India Company (henceforth EIC, or just 'Company'), in this way, sought to learn about Indian history and legal usages. The early academic initiatives by the EIC's administration, as a result, were in the Orientalist framework.

William Jones (1746–94), a judge in the Company's employ and an ardent Sanskritist, founded the Asiatic Society in 1784. A research institute in the contemporary sense, it sought to build a body of knowledge about India and broader Asia (mainly through textual studies). Institutions such as the Calcutta Madrassah, Benaras Sanskrit College, and the College of Fort William (established, respectively, in 1781, 1791, and 1800) run by the Company taught the contemporary Indian languages to its servants and trained Indians for subordinate positions in its legal administration through a classical Arabic, Persian, and Sanskrit education.

The Orientalist education policy of the EIC met a protracted demise in the first half of the 19th century. The gradual buildup of critical scrutiny and hostile campaigns against the Company resulted in the British Parliament depriving it of its monopoly of India trade under the

Charter Act of 1813. The Act also enabled the Christian missionaries to operate in India and made the EIC formally responsible for the instruction of Indians. In the subsequent years, the former became the major purveyors of Western education among Indians. Eventually, the EIC's administration too had to begin providing it in a small way by the start of the 1830s. Apparently, this was in response to the emergent public mood in favour of English medium Western education (since it opened up job prospects) and the demands of the reformist Indian elites. A section in the Company's General Committee of Public Instruction, today remembered as the 'Anglicists', was also pushing for it aggressively. They ultimately triumphed as Thomas Babington Macaulay (1800–59) came to head this committee. A lengthy note, or 'minute', penned by him in 1835 ensured that the Company abandoned the Orientalist education policy for good.

Then, in 1853, Charles Wood (1800–85), another high-ranking official, wrote a 'despatch' that finalized the administrative and institutional framework of education in the EIC's Indian territories. His objective was of course to promote a Western curriculum. In the remainder of the 19th century, while its Western content was a settled fact, there was the retreat of both missionary and governmental agency in the colonial education scene. The Christian proselytizers had apparently lost their earlier enthusiasm for educational initiatives as these had not won them a significant number of converts. The colonial administration too was wary of backing the missionaries since it did not wish to risk a repeat of the uprising of 1857 by offending Indian religious sensibilities. As we note, while the government retained control over the lower rungs of the education system, it encouraged Indian initiative at the secondary and collegiate levels. Indians seized the chance and soon overtook the missionaries in the field of college education. Thus, circumstances converged in such a way that a determinately Indian and Hindu intervention in Indian higher education was now possible, even necessary (on account of the perishing of native education). As it turned out, Malaviya, because of his unique personality and cultivation, became the chief author of this intervention. He envisioned it in a way that it fitted into the contemporary structure of Indian higher academia, based on Western curriculum, and represented the intellectual heritage of the land. Malaviya, in this way, became the main architect of a university that represented, as we shall term it, the dialogic discourse of Indian modernity.

Chapter 2 attempts to contextualize Malaviya's conception of a Hindu university in terms of his personal background and conduct in public life. He was, as we shall see, from an orthodox Brahmin family of great traditional learning. His early schooling was in the traditional framework as well. He appears to have received it in institutions which were the surviving vestiges of native schooling. At a later point, however, Malaviya moved to a school that imparted a Western curriculum. Thereafter, he earned a BA degree at Muir Central College in Allahabad. Although he had to abandon his postgraduate studies due to the paucity of funds, Malaviya eventually did an LLB at Allahabad University.

Malaviya's family background and education thus made him an individual with great catholicity of outlook. He was a traditional Hindu pandit who had also received the best liberal arts education that British-ruled India could provide. Malaviya's personality represented a mixture of the best of

Indian and Western learning. He brought his catholicity of outlook to public life. As a member of the Indian National Congress, Malaviya was a liberal constitutionalist who tried his best to leverage the representative institutions of the colonial state to bring succour to his compatriots. He was a politician who eschewed rigid, dogmatic positions. At the same time, Malaviya was a Hindu activist who passionately advocated causes relevant to the dignity and welfare of his co-religionists. He, however, never showed the slightest animus towards non-Hindus.

Malaviya's educational vision was social democratic, since he was partly a liberal. He considered a basic school level education everyone's right and the key to social welfare and national advancement. Malaviya also wanted education to be culturally rooted. Nevertheless, he fully understood that it must have technical and scientific content. Malaviya's educational philosophy was well-rounded and holistic. It melded the seeming opposites, just as he combined a commitment to liberal constitutionalism with Hindu activism in public life.

Malaviya's educational philosophy had an obvious reflection in his conception of a Hindu university. In the prospectus he drafted in 1905, he imagined it as an institution that would preserve and impart traditional Indian knowledge and also provide the latest technical and scientific education.

Chapter 3 is an account of the conflicting and evolving visions, interpersonal drama, activism, and politics that culminated in the passing of the Banaras Hindu University Bill in the Imperial Legislative Council on 1 October 1915. Along with Malaviya, the chief protagonists in this part of the book are his allies Annie Besant (1847–1933) and the

Maharaja of Darbhanga, Rameshwar Singh (1860–1929), as well as the colonial in charge of education, Sir Harcourt Butler (1869–1938).

The first three decades of the Banaras Hindu University (BHU) are the focus of Chapter 4. It looks at the institution's controversy marred inauguration, struggles through instability in the higher administrative echelons and financial insolvency, vibrant and eclectic academics (a combination of traditional learning, the most cutting-edge disciplines, and physical education), and penchant for nationalist agitation. The chapter also highlights BHU's attempts to architecturally project its denominational identity, provide religious instruction without coercion, combine education in Hindu moral values and 'communitas' with moral and intellectual freedom (students were free to follow Marx or Gandhi even if Malaviya personally disagreed), and the tension and interplay between orthodoxy and reformism in its functioning. Thus, in certain ways, Chapter 4 examines BHU's attempts to balance tradition and its role as a mainly Western-style institution of higher education and captures its overall dialogic nature.

The final chapter goes over the noteworthy episodes at the institution post-independence, and finally documents the Congress ruled centre's attempt to rename it 'Madan Mohan Malaviya Kashi Vishwavidyalaya' in 1965. Undertaken in the name of secularism, BHU students conducted a massive agitation against the move until it fell through in the Lok Sabha. Thus, the end point of this book is about a tumultuous confrontation between the dialogic modernity embodied by BHU and a rigidly Western-inspired enterprise in secularism. We, in this way, survey BHU's course from its inception to crisis.

1

The Century before BHU: Education in Colonial India

Colonial Knowledge and the Orientalist Education Policy

Incorporated in 1600 as a mercantile firm and commencing its operations in India not long thereafter,[1] the EIC eventually ended up as a territorial power. Over the 18th century, it inexorably ascended militarily (a history that need not detain us here), first prevailing over its principal European rival, the French East India Company (in the Carnatic Wars), and then some major Indian powers. The EIC also acquired, at the same time, extensive territories in the east, south, and west of India. Ruling them meant establishing formal frameworks of administration and the EIC set about to do just that. By and by, thus, in the closing decades of the 18th century and the early ones of the 19th, the EIC set up a judicial, land revenue, and police administration in its domains.

Simultaneously, the EIC undertook a major knowledge-gathering exercise and sought a deeper understanding of India. This was, of course, to ensure the efficacy and smooth functioning of its administration with the relevant data and information. The officials of the EIC, in this way, began to build, what we shall term, a body of 'colonial knowledge' about what was for them a largely unfamiliar social world. The anthropologist B.S. Cohn calls this enterprise an 'investigative modality', involving the 'definition of a [required] body of information', the procedures of its acquisition, and its subsequent transformation into 'usable forms such as published reports, statistical returns, histories, gazetteers, legal codes, and encyclopedias'.[2]

The colonial 'investigative modality' also had a historiographic side to it. Cohn terms it a 'historiographic modality'.[3] This was a moment in their encounter with India when the British, so to speak, were in the process of seeking answers to some very fundamental questions about the country through historical inquiries. They sought to know, for instance, who the Indians were (seemingly in terms of historical origins) and what was their place 'among the nations of the world'.[4] To a considerable extent, as it appears to us, the British attempted to answer these questions at this juncture through textual studies, or, rather, by undertaking translations of classical language Indian texts. For example, *The Code of Gentoo Laws* was prepared by Nathaniel Brassey Halhed (1751–1830), an official of the EIC, in 1776 from a 'Persian translation of a Sanskrit digest of Hindu law'.[5] The Persian text had been commissioned from several Brahmins by the EIC. A few years prior, in 1768, Alexander Dow (1735–79), another Company man, had published *The History of Hindostan*. The work was the translation of a history written in Persian by Firishta (1570–1620).[6] The colonial 'investigative modality,' in this way, ventured into 'Orientalist' territory, or a field of learning primarily centering around the study of classical Eastern

('Oriental') languages such as Sanskrit, Persian, and Arabic. The Orientalist proclivity of the colonial 'investigative modality' eventually received a major fillip through, as we shall term it, the first significant academic initiative by the EIC. This was the Asiatic Society, established in Calcutta (now Kolkata) in 1784 by William Jones, a judge in the EIC's judicial administration. Jones, as the historian Thomas Trautmann puts it, was 'a prodigy of Orientalism'[7] and is chiefly remembered today for his translations of Kalidasa's *Shakuntala* and the *Manusmriti*. These were respectively published as *The Sacontala: Or, The Fatal Ring* and *The Institutes of Hindu Law: Or, the Ordinances of Menu* in the years 1789 and 1796.

In the contemporary sense, the Asiatic Society was a research institute whose objective was the promotion of learning about India and the rest of Asia (chiefly through textual studies). It continues to exist in this form today. Commenced in 1788, the Society journal, *Asiatick Researches*, was a 'great hit' in Europe,[8] presumably due to the rising curiosity about the non-Western world within the learned circles there.

Just as the Asiatic Society, the second major academic initiative by the EIC also bore a pronouncedly Orientalist character. The College of Fort William was started in Calcutta in 1800, while Lord Wellesley (1760–1842) was the Governor-General of the EIC's territories. The objective behind the founding of the institution was the training of the Company's personnel. The EIC employed large numbers of 'writers', or clerks, some of them 'British lads as young as fifteen',[9] who, it seems, arrived in India wholly ignorant of its languages. By the end of the 18th century, the extent of the EIC's administration had become quite considerable.

With this had grown, as we understand, its need for staff who were better trained in the way of familiarity with Indian languages. After all, the EIC was ruling such large numbers of Indians now. Thus, the EIC's 'writers' were taught a three-year course at the College of Fort William before being sent off to their desks at various locations in its territories.

The course's focus was mainly on the languages. As we learn from Trautmann, it comprised three classical languages, namely, Sanskrit, Persian, and Arabic, and six 'modern languages', namely, Hindustani, Bengali, Telugu, Marathi, Tamil, and Kannada.[10] The first professors at the College of Fort William came from the Asiatic Society. These were, of course, British. Several Indians were appointed too at the institution. They were either assistants for language teaching,[11] or worked as munshis and pandits and produced books in Indian languages for the instruction of the 'writers'. The latter is the reason why modern Indian prose, to some extent, took shape at the College of Fort William. For instance, some of the earliest prose works in Bengali were produced there by the likes of Ramram Basu (1751–1813), Chandicharan Munshi (1760–1808), and Mrityunjay Vidyalankar (1762–1819).[12] Along with traditional classroom-based pedagogy (that presumably used the texts produced by Indian munshis and pandits), scholars at the College of Fort William acquired felicity in Indian languages through 'disputations' or debates. For example, on 6 February 1806, debates in three languages, namely, Persian, Bengali, and Hindustani were conducted at the institution. The topics, respectively, were as follows: 'An academical institution in India, is advantageous to the Natives, and to the British Nation'; 'The Asiatics are capable of as high a degree of civilization, as the Europeans'; and 'The Hindoostanee [sic] Language is the most generally useful in India'.[13] Once the debates concluded and the prizes were given away, Sir George Barlow (1763–1846),[14] 'the Honorable Acting Visitor' (chief guest?), delivered an address in which, among other things, he noted how the College of Fort William had 'extended a general attention to the Oriental languages, literature, and knowledge, which … [promised] to be productive of the most salutary effects in the administration … of the Honorable Company in India'.[15] In other words, the gentleman noted the institution's efficacy in furthering the EIC's 'governmentality'[16] through Orientalist learning.

The EIC had preceded the College of Fort William with a couple of collegiate institutions oriented towards 'native' society. These were also projects in governmentality. The Calcutta Madrassah was founded in 1781 under the Governor-Generalship of Warren Hastings for the promotion of Arabic and Persian scholarship. The Benaras Sanskrit College was established a decade later by Jonathan Duncan, a resident of the holy city. It was, as the name indicates, focused on imparting Sanskrit learning. Both institutions were meant to train Indians to assist the EIC's judges in understanding the principles of Muslim and Hindu jurisprudence.

The courts established by the EIC in its domains had turned out to be rather disruptive and unpopular since they followed English legal principles that often militated against Indian social conventions. Eventually, the Amending Act of 1781[17] mandated that 'inheritance and succession to lands, rents, and goods, and all matters of contract and dealing between party and party' shall be arbitrated on the basis of Muslim or Hindu legal usages if they happened to be

Muslim or Hindu by religion.[18] The Calcutta Madrassah and the Benaras Sanskrit College, thus, were created as 'nurseries' of 'doctors and expounders'[19] of these usages who would be absorbed into the EIC's legal administration and render it palatable to Indians.

The two institutions may be seen as expressions of the EIC's Orientalist education policy towards Indian society. This meant that it thought it prudent to abjure supporting the missionaries who wanted to promote Western learning in India, while also not promoting it itself. Instead, the EIC tried to emulate the patronage traditionally extended by Hindu and Muslim rulers to Sanskrit and Arabic education.[20] Thus, at the cusp of the 18th and 19th centuries, as the EIC's own cognitive efforts regarding India were mainly based on classical studies, it was seeking to patronize and undergird the same within Indian society.

The EIC's Indifference towards Mass Instruction

While the Asiatic Society was a research institute, the College of Fort William was, might we say, a staff training institute. The Calcutta Madrassah and the Benaras Sanskrit College, on the other hand, were chiefly meant to supply the EIC with a suitable pool of potential lower-level native functionaries (which again makes them initiatives in staff training). These early academic initiatives on the part of the EIC did not have an implication for Indian society at large since they were not, so to speak, generally pitched at it.

Essentially, the Asiatic Society and the College of Fort William were the EIC's attempts at self-education so that it ruled India more efficiently. The Calcutta Madrassah and the Benaras Sanskrit College did cater to Indians, but not in the way of mass instruction. These institutions imparted a classical education which was useful to a very small, elite segment of the Indian society in terms of earning a livelihood. As a matter of fact, it is very likely that the EIC sought to 'win the confidence' of upper-class Indians and 'consolidate its rule in India'[21] by training their sons for employment in its judicial administration at the Calcutta Madrassah and the Benaras Sanskrit College.

Speaking of educational institutions potentially of general relevance and utility, the EIC was running a number of 'charity schools' in its garrisons and around its 'factories' since the early years of the 18th century (after it was directed to do so under the Charter Act of 1698).[22] But their scope was very limited, and they were very few in number (five in Madras, one in Calcutta, and another in Bombay). The charity schools were generally meant for the children born of the EIC's English soldiers' marital unions with Indian women. Sometimes, they admitted 'a few orphan and poor Indian children'.[23] Along with financial grants from the EIC, the charity schools ran on 'donations from philanthropic and religious persons'.[24] The very fact that a part of their operational costs were met through largesse indicates that they were not much of a priority for the EIC, it did not even bother to fund them fully. The Company, as it seems, was quite casual in its approach towards these institutions since it was not yet interested in creating its own system of mass instruction in India. This is not surprising since such a system barely existed in Britain at this point. The EIC could not have undertaken an initiative whose need was yet to be felt in its home country.

England, as Dharampal writes in *The Beautiful Tree*, an extremely significant work of scholarship on indigenous schooling in early colonial India, 'had few schools for the children of ordinary people till about 1800'.[25] School education 'at the people's level', in this way, we learn, was an 'uncommon commodity' in the country at the turn of the 19th century.[26] As a matter of fact, it appears to have been anything but universal even in the upper stratum of English society. Thus, even a very expensive 'public' (that is, private) school like Shrewsbury, writes Dharampal, did not have more than 'three or four boys' in 1797.[27] Later, 'after some major reorganization', we are told, it came to teach about twenty students annually,[28] still a very inconsiderable number.

The curriculum at the upscale schools of England was again as modest as their apparent intake of scholars. At Eton, one observes, 'teaching consisted of writing and arithmetic',[29] with some 'ancient Geography, or algebra' thrown in at a later stage (in the fifth form). A pupil had to stay at the institution 'long enough' to be introduced to a 'part of' Euclid.[30] This must mean, as it appears, that no geometry at all was taught in the lower forms there. One is also tempted to wonder about the level and amount of the arithmetic imparted at Eton, since mathematics became a part of the regular schoolwork in England only in 1851.[31] The nondescript curriculum at Eton at the end of the 18th century is more striking in view of the fact that it catered to the wards of the English aristocracy. The contemporary schools instructing the children of the average English men and women (whatever few did exist), very likely, did not fare better in terms of their academics. It seems safe to hazard the guess that they might have fared worse.

The 'Beautiful Tree'

In marked contrast to England, contemporary India appears to have had a widespread network of schools serving a considerable cross section of society. This is indicated by what survived of indigenous schooling in India in the first half of the nineteenth century. In 1822, for instance, Thomas Munro (1761–1827), the Governor of the Madras Presidency, reckoned that there was a school for every 500 persons in the territory under his charge. Further, he estimated that about a third of the males received schooling in the native population he oversaw.[32] The social coverage of indigenous schooling in early colonial South India, thus, appears to have been rather appreciable. In terms of its content too this schooling was seemingly quite adequate, as we gather from an account in an anonymous Collector's report. Bidden to study the native schools in Bellary, the district he was administering, by Munro, the Collector observed that the scholars were first imparted a very 'thorough' knowledge of the alphabet. Thereafter, he saw that they were taught to write the 'compounds' (the syllables that split and combine the consonants or vowels and consonants) and instructed, among other things, in the multiplication tables, fractions, integers, 'and the three-fold measures of capacity, weight and extent'. The scholars would also write 'common letters', learn to draw 'forms of agreement', read 'fables and legendary tables [sic]', and commit 'various kinds of poetry to memory' to 'attain distinctness and clearness in pronunciation together with readiness and correctness in reading any kind of composition'.[33]

The 'Hindoo [sic] youths', the Collector apprised Munro, generally began their education at the age of five and, depending on their means, stayed in school from five to fourteen or fifteen years.[34] At its fullest extent, in terms of the number of years, it seems, indigenous schooling in the 1820s' Madras Presidency somewhat surpassed modern schooling. Going by the curriculum, those who partook in the entirety of it must have acquired rather more than a practical literacy and quite an advanced level of numeracy. Even more, since, it appears, while at school, they would revise and put to the test what they had learnt by instructing the younger pupils. Our anonymous Collector alludes to this convention at the native schools and terms it 'admirable'. He thought that it gave the senior pupils time to 'confirm their own knowledge'. Apparently, the South Indian practice of senior schoolboys teaching their juniors had inspired certain people in the Collector's home country – we find him remarking that it 'well deserves the imitation it has received in England'.[35]

Overall, it seems, the gentleman was very impressed by the efficacy of indigenous Indian schooling. He also noted how frugal it was, emphasizing in his report the '*economy with which [Indian] children are taught*'.[36]

Like the Collector of Bellary, G.L. Prendergast, a member of the Executive Council of the Governor of the Bombay Presidency, had also come to admire the thrift characterizing native schooling. Besides, he was impressed by its efficacy in the way of imparting a proficient numeracy across social segments. As he wrote in 1821:

> [Y]oung natives are taught reading, writing, and arithmetic upon a system so economical, from a handful or two of grain to perhaps a rupee per month to the schoolmaster, according to the ability of the parents, and at the same time so simple and effectual, that there is hardly a cultivator or petty dealer who is not competent to keep his own accounts with a degree of accuracy … whilst the more splendid dealers and bankers keep their books with … ease, conciseness, and clearness.

Prendergast had also not missed how numerous the native schools were in the Bombay Presidency. As he put it:

> [T]here is hardly a village, great or small, throughout our territories, in which there is not at least one school, and in larger villages [there are] more; many [are] in every town, and in large cities [they are] in every division[37]

The network of indigenous schools, as we see, survived into the next decade. William Adam (1796–1881), 'a zealous missionary',[38] discovered a 'very great' number of them in rural Bengal. These, he noted, provided instruction 'in the elements of knowledge' and were 'supported by the Natives themselves'.[39] Bengal and Bihar taken together, he estimated the number of such schools to be no less than 1,00,000. In the two provinces, reckoned Adam, there was a village school for every 400 people.[40] Apparently, they had the better of the Madras Presidency in terms of the social coverage of schooling. Adam made his estimates based on what he observed at firsthand from 1835 to 1838, after undertaking an enquiry into native education at the behest of Lord William Bentinck (1774–1839), the Governor-General of the EIC's Indian territories.[41] The figures furnished by him are even more telling in light of the fact that he was a Christian proselytizer. It is very unlikely that he might have been inclined in any manner to idealizing or eulogizing Indian society.

Along with their very considerable density, we also see Adam documenting the education that the indigenous schools in eastern India provided. The 'scholars', he reports, were first taught the alphabet – they 'traced the vowels and consonants with the finger on a sand-board with a pencil of steatite or white crayon' for eight or ten days. Thereafter, for 'about a year', informs Adam, they would practice writing 'on the palm-leaf with a reed-pen ... with ink made of charcoal ... joining vowels to the consonants, forming compound letters, syllables, and words, and learning tables of numeration, money, weight, and measure, and the correct mode of writing the distinctive names of persons, castes, and places'. Next, as the missionary writes, the pupils 'advanced to the study of arithmetic', and learnt 'addition, subtraction, multiplication and division, and the simplest cases of mensuration of land and commercial and agricultural accounts, together with the modes of address proper in writing letters to different persons'. Finally, the village schools observed by Adam taught their wards 'agricultural and commercial accounts' and the 'composition of letters'.[42]

These institutions, if one may call them that, operated in informal setups, generally 'in the houses of some of the most respectable native gentlemen'.[43] Typically, it seems, the number of years that rural children spent in them were not too many. They would, so to speak, 'graduate' before attaining puberty. This is expected in a social context in which male children (who, as a rule, are likely to have attended these village schools) would be required to contribute their labour to agricultural work as soon as they were physically capable. Their schooling, thus, could not be too drawn out. In Bengal, as seen by Adam, pupils would commence their lessons at the village schools upon turning five and leave them at the age of ten.[44] The teachers, as he reports, were compensated 'from various sources', a couple of them being donations by philanthropists and the fees paid by the students.[45]

The village schools surveyed by Adam, thus, imparted some optimum, practical literacy and a respectable degree of numeracy to rural children within a relatively short period. In terms of how they were organized and functioned, as we understand, they seem to have been autonomous initiatives by rural communities. These schools were also quite inclusive of their various constituent units or segments in the way of both the 'taught and the teachers'. 'Every caste group' was represented among the former, even the Doms and Chandalas. The schoolmasters' backgrounds were equally diverse. The 'greater proportion' of them did come from the Brahmin, Kayastha, Sadgop, and Aguri jatis, that is, the upper and middle segments of rural society. But there was also the odd Chandala teacher in the rural schools of Bengal and Bihar when Adam studied them.[46]

Going by the testimonies of some colonial administrators and a Christian missionary, indigenous schooling, to a great extent, appears to have survived the establishment of EIC's rule in the south, west, and east of India. It disseminated a reasonably widespread and proficient literacy and numeracy amongst Indians, regardless of social rank or status. The 'beautiful tree', as Dharampal terms it, of indigenous Indian schooling was still standing in the early decades of the 19th century. However, as we shall see, it would wither and perish over its remainder, first through neglect and, eventually, the loss of social patronage caused by the policies of the colonial administration.

The Charter Act of 1813 and Indian Education

We have observed that there was not much in the way of a system of mass instruction in England at the end of the 18th century. This is, apparently, the reason why the EIC was not keen on investing in mass instruction in India. A band of robber merchants could not have prioritized a matter far away in conquered territories which was not yet a priority in their own society. However, by the beginning of the 19th century, the attitude of the English elites towards mass instruction had begun to change. They were now seeing it as an area that required the intervention of the state. The English elites were motivated by a desire to improve the lives of the poor—perhaps to render them more 'productive'—and they chiefly sought to do so by educating them. Founded, respectively, in 1803 and 1808, organizations such as the Sunday School Union and the Royal Lancastrian Institution, thus, came to vigorously advocate the education of the poor.

The issue also came up in the British Parliament in 1807 in the form of a bill tabled by Samuel Whitbread (1764–1815). It proposed free schooling for all children in the seven to fourteen age group and the establishment of schools funded by local taxation. Unfortunately, although passed in the House of Commons, the bill was not ratified in the House of the Lords. Its proposals, thus, were not eventually implemented.[47]

As the English elites came around to the idea that one of the basic welfare functions of the state is the promotion of mass instruction, some of them grew very mindful of the fact that the EIC's administration in India was doing no such thing. In general, as a matter of fact, a conspicuous section of the English intellectual and political class had at this time grown very critical of the EIC's activities in India. They were acutely aware of how the 'Honorable Company' was brazenly despoiling its Indian possessions while spending recklessly on warfare and keenly wanted to bring it under tighter parliamentary control. An especially vocal and conscientious representative of the group was the philosopher and long-standing Whig parliamentarian Edmund Burke (1729–97).[48] He was very certain that the EIC needed 'reformation', and declared as much to his fellow MPs during a debate in 1783.[49] A 'philanthropist, pure and simple', he 'kept the problems of India' constantly in focus and generated a feeling in the House of Commons that it was the 'bounden duty' of His Majesty's Government to look after the 'well-being' of Indians.[50] The House of Commons, of course, did not immediately heed Burke. But he, as we see, ought to be credited for initiating a systematic, critical examination of the EIC's affairs and activities, a scrutiny that would be taken up in the lower house of the British Parliament (even if for reasons of political economy) in the following century.

Along with Burke, Charles Grant (1746–1823) and William Wilberforce (1759–1833), prominent men in English public life, were also eager to help the Indians. Unlike Burke's, their interest in India, however, was mainly evangelical. Both desired to promote Western learning amongst Indians to expedite their Christianization.[51] The more voluble of the two, in the way of contributing to the British perception of India, was Grant. He entered the British Parliament in 1802 and took charge as the Chairman of the EIC in 1805. He had, however, resided in India intermittently since 1767, when he first arrived there as a soldier in the EIC's army.[52] Grant was, in this way, a veteran 'India hand' when he rose to the top in the Honourable Company. He was quite familiar with the country and filled with contempt for it.

Grant was also very candid about this contempt and had eloquently vented it in 1792, when he authored the pamphlet 'Observations on the State of Society among the Asiatic Subjects of Great Britain, particularly with Respect to Morals; and on the Means of Improving it'. It contained, from his point of view, a 'lengthy description of Indian society and the character of the people', especially Hindus. Grant thought 'abandoned selfishness' to be the chief 'distinguishing mark of Hindu character'. Because of this, as he concluded in the 'Observations', 'fraud and deceit' dominated human interactions in India. If the public conduct of Indians was deplorable, in his view, they were no better in their private, familial lives. Grant found both the 'natural affection of parents for children' and 'conjugal love' absent in India. Indian men, as perceived by him, lived unrestrained by morality as 'brutes.' The women, on the other hand, were condemned by a life of 'servitude and semi-imprisonment' to a 'violent and premature death.'[53]

Grant considered Hinduism, the dominant religion of the Indian people, 'vile' and 'morally degrading'. The 'Observations', thus, gave 'graphic descriptions ... of the cruel and licentious gods, and especially of the skull-draped images of Kali.'[54] In summary, one might say, Grant thought of the Hindus as a horrid lot of human beings with an equally horrid religion.

The extremely slanderous tenor of the 'Observations' may be seen as a 'serious attempt to find a sanction for permanent British rule in India' on the part of Grant.[55] He, it seems, thought that the British were entitled to rule the country forever since they possessed a superior spiritual truth in which he himself was a passionate believer, namely, Christianity. Grant, however, did not want the British to hold India through brute force alone. He believed that British power in the country would be permanent if based on 'good government'. Hence, thought Grant, it was especially necessary for the British to efface Hinduism, a 'system of errors that fed upon the miseries of the people'.[56] In other words, this fervent evangelist (a member of the Clapham Sect,[57] no less) believed that the British would demonstrate their sagacity and charitable nature as a ruling power if they rid India of the Hindu religion. Hence, his interest in giving a Western education in the English language to Hindus. Grant thought it to be a sure way of dissuading them from their own religious beliefs and bring them into Christianity. He rhetorically prescribed in the Observations,

> The true cure of darkness is the introduction of light. The Hindoos [sic] err, because they are ignorant; and their errors have never fairly been laid before them. The communication of ... light and knowledge to them would prove the best remedy for their disorders.[58]

Grant was very optimistic about Hindus being able to acquire the English language and wanted it to be imparted to them 'by degrees' through 'easy literary compositions, upon a variety of subjects'. The 'Observations', thus, recommended that the EIC's administration 'establish, at moderate expense, in various parts of the Provinces, places of gratuitous instruction in reading and writing English'.[59]

Wilberforce wore multiple hats. He was a philanthropist who was chiefly known for his abolitionist, or anti-slavery, advocacy. Alongside, he was a politician who was elected an MP in 1780. Finally, Wilberforce, like Grant, was a Clapham Sect evangelist. He, as we learn, became interested in Indian affairs soon after becoming a parliamentarian. In 1793, when the EIC's Charter was up for renewal at the Palace of

Westminster, the following resolution was initiated in and carried through the House of Commons by Wilberforce:

> That it is the peculiar and bounden duty of the British Legislature to promote by all just and prudent means the interest and happiness of the British Dominions in India; and that for these ends such measures ought to be adopted as may gradually tend to their advancement in useful knowledge and to their religious and moral improvement.

As the phrases 'useful knowledge' and 'religious and moral improvement' seem to indicate, the resolution urged the British Parliament to promote Western learning in India and, through its means, the Christianization of Indians.[60]

Wilberforce's resolution was 'violently' opposed by the EIC's Court of Directors. As we already know, the EIC was not interested in undertaking the large-scale instruction of Indians at this juncture. Neither was the conversion of India to Christianity a priority for the Company brass. These gentlemen believed that the 'faith and morals' of the Hindus were as good as those of any other people. Thus, they warned, any attempt to convert them or 'give them any more learning or any other description of learning than what they already possessed' would be 'madness'.[61] The Court of Directors, in other words, took the pragmatic view that the EIC ought not to unnecessarily aggrieve the Indians by challenging their usages and beliefs. They must have feared a violent backlash and a potential disruption of the Honourable Company's pursuit of riches. The British Parliament, it seems, agreed and ignored the recommendations of Wilberforce's resolution. Thus, it did not press the executive authority to carry them out.

The evangelical lobby at the Palace of Westminster (which Wilberforce was apparently leading), in this way, was defeated. However, as it eventually turned out, this defeat was not permanent.

Over the next two decades, as the Industrial Revolution took off in England, the EIC increasingly earned the enmity of a very important segment of the English public. Simultaneously, the Honourable Company lost friends and allies in the British Parliament because of making repeated and enormous demands on the national exchequer. As a mercantile firm that was a net importer of goods from India, it had become something of an eyesore and an anachronism in the context of the contemporary English political economy. That it enjoyed a monopoly over India trade did not help matters either. The owners of industry across England now wanted to secure the home market against Indian manufacturing, especially cotton textiles (which formed the bulk of the EIC's imports). Alongside, they wanted unhindered access to the Indian market (which the EIC's monopoly denied to them). The English manufacturing interest, as a result, got vocally opposed to the EIC. It found its protagonists in a section of the political class which was tired of the EIC's profligate military adventures and periodic appeals to Parliament for financial bailouts. Consequently, it became common for MPs to decry the EIC in some way or another. For instance, on 3 July 1812, a certain Mr Creevey rose in the House of Commons to call the EIC's monopoly over India trade a 'monstrous national grievance'. He appealed to the government to listen to the 'loud and general voice of the commercial interests' and rescind this monopoly.[62] Before long, this 'loud and general voice' was inveighing against the EIC and demanding the establishment of a free-trade regime with India through parliamentary petitions. For example, the petition from the 'merchants, and manufacturers of Manchester and Salford' was read out in the House of Commons on 3 February 1813. The establishment of 'an open commercial intercourse,' it argued,

> [G]enerally with the countries from which the existing charter [issued to the EIC] excludes the British merchants, would not only afford the most effectual relief in the present situation of public affairs, but would … most essentially contribute to the lasting benefit and prosperity of the kingdom at large.[63]

The same day, another petition from 'several merchants, traders and other inhabitants of the city of Bristol' was heard in the House of Commons. Rather more passionate in tone, it declared:

> [T]he full and free right to trade to and with all countries and people in amity with their sovereign, and more particularly with those countries and settlements acquired and maintained by the efforts and valour of the forces of his Majesty, is the undoubted birthright and inheritance of the people of this empire; and that the exclusive privilege of the E.I. Company is a manifest infringement of that right.[64]

The House of Commons did not take long to respond to these pleas, indicating that it was dominantly ill-disposed towards the EIC. On 22 March 1813, it appointed a 'committee of the whole House' to examine the EIC's affairs and review the many petitions received regarding its 'trade and shipping.'[65] Then, on 14 April, the House of Commons followed up by appointing a 'Select Committee' to 'facilitate the progress' of the committee of the 'whole House'.[66] The Select Committee moved quickly. On 3 June, it tabled a resolution in the House of Commons recommending that the government allow all subjects of Great Britain to export 'any goods, wares, or merchandize' to the ports till then exclusively reserved for the operations of the EIC.[67] In effect, this meant that the Select Committee sought to open the Indian ports to the British commercial class at large and deprive the EIC of its monopoly over India trade.

The House of Commons acted with remarkable alacrity after this. It passed the 'East India Company Charter Bill,' or the 'Charter Act of 1813,' on 13 July and rescinded the EIC's more than two centuries' old exclusive right with regards to India trade. Additionally, the lower house of the British Parliament used the Act to significantly circumscribe the EIC's autonomy as a territorial power in India, very likely to check its proclivity for waging war and make it answerable to the metropole in administrative matters. The EIC's Indian possessions were thus brought under the 'undoubted sovereignty of the Crown of the United Kingdom'.[68] Interestingly, along with the commercial, political, and administrative matters pertaining to the EIC, the Charter Act of 1813 also took in its purview the need 'to promote the interests and happiness of the native inhabitants of the British dominions in India ... [for which] measures ought to be adopted as may tend to the introduction among them of useful knowledge and moral improvement'.

The Act laid down that 'in furtherance of the above objects, sufficient facilities shall be afforded by law to persons desirous of going to, or remaining in, India for the purpose of accomplishing these benevolent designs'.[69]

It also mandated that the Company's administration set aside

> a sum of not less than one lac of rupees in each year … [for] the revival and improvement of literature and the encouragement of the learned natives of India, and for the introduction and promotion of a knowledge of the sciences among the inhabitants of the British territories in India.[70]

The Charter Act of 1813, in this way, expressed the House of Common's seeming interest in the social and intellectual advancement of the Indians. The overall implications of the Charter Act of 1813 for the Indian educational scene were nothing less than momentous. First, it paved the way for Christian missionaries to freely work and reside in the EIC's Indian territories, as they could clearly qualify as persons interested in the dissemination of 'useful knowledge' among Indians as well as their 'moral improvement'. This meant that, if they desired, Christian missionaries could now establish schools in India. Second, the Act, for the first time, made the EIC formally responsible for the education of Indians through a systematic budgetary allocation. The Company, as a result, was quite unprecedentedly stirred into debating and explicitly spelling out a policy framework regarding education in its Indian domains.

Why was the House of Commons suddenly interested in improving the Indians' lot in social and intellectual terms? It is possible that this unprecedented behaviour on its part was inspired by what the likes of Burke, Grant, and Wilberforce had advocated for India two or three decades earlier. Perhaps the honourable MPs were hearkening to their exhortations as they sought to trammel the EIC and advance the proselytization and instruction of Indians. However, it is equally likely that the British political establishment was, at this point, driven by the logic of political economy in its apparent bid to re-engineer Indian society and its spiritual and cognitive frameworks. As it opened the Indian market to the English industrial and commercial class at large, the House of Commons might have wanted Indians to become enthusiastic consumers of English manufactures. Hence, perhaps, its interest in transforming the overall Indian mentalité through Christianization and hopefully (provided that the EIC chose to impart it along with the missionaries) Anglicizing education. If successfully achieved, it might have led Indians to culturally identify with the metropole and readily embrace its material goods while not minding their country being leveraged as its economic periphery. One hazards this guess, since, from a purely economic point of view, the Charter Act of 1813 began to shift the colonial relationship between Great Britain and India to the 'liberal' or capitalist framework from the mercantile. In the former, the metropole economically exploits the colony chiefly by using it as a captive market for its manufactured goods and a cheap source of raw materials. This is exactly how it eventually came to be between Great Britain and India. The less sophisticated, mercantile framework of colonial exploitation is characterized by the direct plunder of native society as a whole and the extraction of tribute payments from its ruling elites through the exercise of military power. This had been the EIC's way, now grown unpopular with the political class back home due to the, so to speak, enormous 'overheads' involved (in the form of military expenditure, which often nullified the apparent gains). The Company's old manner of exploiting India would now become increasingly marginal.[71]

Demise of the Orientalist Education Policy

If the honourable MPs had hoped that the EIC would immediately revise its education policy and base it on a Western curriculum because of the Charter Act of 1813, they were disappointed. The Company brass was, instead, divided on the matter of how to most efficiently further the education of Indians in its aftermath. This was because the Act had left it unexplained as to what 'the revival and improvement of literature' and 'the introduction and promotion of a knowledge of the sciences' might mean in the Indian situation in terms of the medium of instruction and curriculum. Since it was so imprecise in its instructions, the senior officials in the Company's administration in Bengal thought that the Orientalist education policy (implicitly adopted by the EIC in the previous century) may be continued with. This group, thus, advocated the promotion of Sanskrit and Arabic learning as before. They even wanted Western science and knowledge to be imparted in these classical languages. Then, there was a second group of high-ranking Company men in the Bombay Presidency who thought it best to make modern Indian languages the medium of instruction in India (regardless, as one imagines, of whether the curriculum was mainly Western or based on indigenous knowledge). The likes of Thomas Munro and Mountstuart Elphinstone (1779–1859) were the most prominent representatives of this idea.[72] The latter, however, as we observe, was not entirely disinclined to extending patronage to a purely classical education either. For instance, Elphinstone oversaw the establishment of Poona Sanskrit College as the Governor of the Bombay Presidency in 1821.[73]

The third, and ultimately triumphant, group of Company men were those in agreement with Grant. They wanted to promote Western learning among Indians through the medium of English. Generally, these were younger officials in the Company's administration.[74] It is likely that they, like their inspiration, viewed India as a benighted land in the throes of heathenism which urgently needed to be 'saved.'

If one excludes the Poona Sanskrit College, it took the EIC nearly a decade to act on the mandate of the Charter Act of 1813 and get down to academic initiatives in an organized fashion. The General Committee of Public Instruction was created in the Bengal Presidency in 1823. Its undertakings, one observes, were in the Orientalist framework. This was because it comprised senior Company hands many of whom were Orientalist scholars in their own right.[75] Over the next ten years, the Committee 'reorganized' the Calcutta Madrassah and the Benaras Sanskrit College, established a Sanskrit College in Calcutta (in 1824), began one Oriental College each in Agra and Delhi, published Sanskrit and Arabic works 'on a large scale', and 'employed Oriental scholars to translate English books containing useful knowledge into the Oriental classical languages'.[76]

However, it is likely that the EIC's top management was reconsidering the Orientalist approach towards the instruction of Indians all this while. In fact, a mere year after the Committee was formed, the Honourable Company's Court of Directors issued a 'despatch' criticizing its work. The document termed the establishment of 'seminaries for the purpose of teaching mere Hindoo [sic] or mere Mahomedan literature' as an exercise in imparting 'a great deal of what was frivolous, not a little of what was purely mischievous and a small remainder indeed in which utility was in any way concerned'.[77] Simply put, the Company's leadership thought that Hindu or Muslim (that is, Sanskrit or Arabic) learning was bereft of any value whatsoever.

The emergent reformist Indian view was also not very amenable to the Orientalist education policy. It was most articulately represented by Raja Ram Mohan Roy (1772–1833). Strongly opposed to the promotion of Sanskrit learning, and inclined towards more 'practical' knowledge, he sent the following missive to the Governor-General, Lord Amherst (1773–1857), in 1823:

> If it had been intended to keep the British nation in ignorance of real knowledge, the Baconian philosophy would not have been allowed to displace the system of the schoolmen, which was the best calculated to perpetuate ignorance. In the same manner, the Sanskrit system of education would be the best calculated to keep this country in darkness, if such had been the policy of the British legislature. But as the improvement of the native population is the object of the Government, it will consequently promote a more liberal and enlightened system of instruction embracing Mathematics, Natural Philosophy, Chemistry, Anatomy, with other useful sciences, which may be accomplished with the sums proposed by employing a few gentlemen of talent and learning, educated in Europe and providing a college furnished with necessary books, implements and other apparatus.[78]

Roy, in other words, thought that a classical Indian education contained nothing enlightening and wanted the Company to build an institution where Indians would be imparted a Western curriculum by, as it seems, European teachers (since no Indians had yet travelled to Europe for education). His advocacy of Western education was not restricted to homilies directed at the rulers alone. We do not know whether this was before or after he wrote the above letter to the Governor-General, but in 1823 Roy founded an English-medium school in Calcutta which he funded himself.[79]

Earlier, in 1816, he had collaborated with the Scottish watchmaker turned educationist David Hare (1775–1842) to conceive of an educational institution wherein 'the youth of his country' would be instructed 'in the science and literature of Europe'. This idea, apparently, was taken up by Sir Hyde East (1764–1847), the Chief Justice of the Supreme Court in Calcutta. He mobilized around it the 'leading members of the Hindu community'[80] in the capital of the EIC's Indian empire so that the Hindu College (today, Presidency University) came into existence in 1817. The very first Indian-led initiative in Western-style higher education, thus, had something to do with Roy in the way of inspiration. Again, more than a decade later, in 1830, Roy would provide his support and cooperation to the Scottish missionary Alexander Duff (1806–78) when he arrived in India to open an English-medium school. He, as we learn, secured a building to house Duff's institution as well as the 'first batch of half a dozen students'[81] for it. In due course, Duff's school became the Scottish Church College. Roy, it seems, favoured Western education to the extent that he was indifferent to the agency providing it.

As far as he was concerned, one imagines, it did not matter if it was the EIC's administration or a Christian proselytizer.

A proselytizer like Duff was fortunate to find an ally in an influential upper-class Indian. Christian missionaries arriving in India typically did not have this advantage. Nevertheless, the general lack of collaborators among the native elites notwithstanding, the two decades following the Charter Act of 1813 saw some intense missionary activity in India in the field of education. The London Missionary Society, the Church Missionary Society, the Wesleyan Mission, and the Scotch Missionary Society all established 'mission stations' in various parts of the country during this period. Generally, as we learn, 'educational activities were almost invariably connected with every mission station'.[82] A considerable number of mission schools seem to have come up across India in this way. The first significant non-Indian effort towards mass instruction in the country, thus, was by the Christian proselytizers and not the EIC regime. The latter was apparently still not very enthusiastic about setting up its own network of schools. This is indicated by the very lackadaisical response of the administration of the Madras Presidency regarding Munro's proposal (mooted in 1826) that one school be set up in each Tahsildary and fifteen in each Collectorate.[83] Munro passed away in 1827, and by 1830 only seventy Tahsildary schools had been started in the Presidency.[84] The colonial administration was clearly not very keen on the project, and it was effectively given up by 1836.[85] Mass instruction was not yet a priority for the EIC. For the Christian missionaries, however, it was so from the very start.

Missionary work in education was, of course, not disinterested. For proselytizers, it was a means to secure converts. Hence, they emerged as the most ardent champions of Western education. This was because of the belief, generally nurtured in missionary circles in India, that instruction in English language and science 'would be inevitably followed by conversion to Christianity'.[86] The missionaries, like Grant, obviously thought that Western learning would undermine Hindu beliefs and cause the natives to embrace 'Christian truth' in large numbers. Beside imparting Western education to Indians, missionaries also took a keen interest in Indian languages. In fact, teaching in the early mission schools was done in the mother tongues of Indians. The missionaries also composed grammars of Indians languages and translated the Bible into them. All this, again, was with the proselytizing intent. The missionaries mostly dealt with the relatively lower strata of Indian society, who typically spoke and understood only their own languages. They, thus, sought to communicate with them more effectively to advance their Christianization.

The missionary network of schools, as we saw, expanded rather quickly. The obvious zeal of the proselytizers apart, this could be because the education provided by them found willing takers. Indians might not have been very enthusiastic about the gospel, but they did, it seems, send their children to mission-run schools when it was an option. This, in turn, causes us to think that a section of Indians had by now begun to see both merit and utility in Western education, very possibly since it inculcated a knowledge of the English language. As the tongue of the new rulers of India, the political value of English was unmistakable. It, in other words, carried the charge of power. Besides, and more importantly, a knowledge of English opened prospects within the colonial administration. It could be, in this way, a means to greater economic security in the form of steady employment (even if in a very lowly position under the white masters) and enhanced social prestige. Something like a public mood, thus, it seems, was emerging in India in favour of an English-medium Western education. As about the Indian elites, the reformists among them were, of course, veritably besotted with the supposed value of a Western style curriculum. We already have before us the instance of Raja Ram Mohun Roy. Such elites were even taking a formal, organizational approach towards the promotion of Western education and English-medium instruction. The Bombay Native Education Society, to give an example, was formed in 1824 and energetically championed the cause of Western education in the Bombay Presidency. It also set up English-medium schools in Bombay, Thane, Panvel, and Pune.[87]

The colonial administration apparently registered the emergent public mood and heeded the reformist viewpoint. By 1833, thus, the General Committee of Public Instruction began English classes at the Oriental College in Agra and the Calcutta Madrassah. Further, 'district English schools' were established in Delhi and Banaras.[88] Meanwhile, the British Parliament passed the Charter Act of 1833. Its provisions mainly mandated certain adjustments in the overall organization of the EIC's Indian administration. However, even though the Act contained no instructions as such regarding the education policy of the EIC, one of its clauses had the effect of bringing about a paradigmatic shift in it. The Charter Act of 1833 added a Law Member to the Executive Council of the Governor-General, perhaps to enhance its general competency regarding legal administration. Subsequently, in 1834, a gentleman named Thomas Babington Macaulay was appointed to this office. He was a firm believer in the supremacy of Western civilization.

Upon arriving in India, Macaulay was also appointed the President of the General Committee of Public Instruction. As things stood, the votaries of Orientalist education had ceased to dominate and control the Committee. These 'Orientalists,' as we call them today, were being challenged by younger Committee members who advocated a Western curriculum in the English medium, or the 'Anglicists.' The ten-member Committee was in a state of impasse, apparently because neither party had the numerical advantage. Both comprised five members each.[89] In the end, it fell upon Macaulay to settle the dispute between them.[90]

On 2 February 1835, Macaulay arbitrated the controversy between the Orientalists and the Anglicists in favour of the latter through a 'minute' or note. Early in this text, he brusquely dismissed the languages spoken by the common Indian masses as too unsophisticated, epistemically bereft, and unworthy of being mediums of instruction:

> [T]he dialects commonly spoken among the natives of ... India contain neither literary nor scientific information, and are moreover so poor and rude that, until they are enriched from some other quarter, it will not be easy to translate any valuable work into them ... the intellectual improvement of those classes of the [Indian] people who have the means of pursuing higher studies can at present be effected only by means of some language not vernacular amongst them.[91]

Subsequently, the minute launched into an unabashedly brash praise of the English language:

> The claims of our own language it is hardly necessary to recapitulate. It stands pre-eminent even among the languages of the West. It abounds with works of imagination not inferior to the noblest which Greece has bequeathed to us with models of every species of eloquence, with historical compositions which, considered merely as narratives, have seldom been surpassed, and which, considered merely as vehicles of ethical and political instruction, have never been equalled, with just and lively representations of human life and human nature, with the most profound speculations on metaphysics, morals, government, jurisprudence, trade, with full and correct information respecting every experimental science which tends to preserve the health, to increase the comfort, or to expand the intellect of man.[92]

While English, according to Macaulay, was rich in knowledge of every description, the classical Oriental languages merely abounded in fantastical nonsense:

> The question now before us is simply whether, when it is in our power to teach this language, we shall teach languages in which by universal confession, there are no books on any subject which deserve to be compared to our own, whether when we can teach European science, we shall teach systems which, by universal confession, wherever they differ from those of Europe, differ for the worse, and whether, when we can patronize sound philosophy and true history, we shall countenance, at the public expense, medical doctrines which would disgrace an English farrier, astronomy which would move laughter in girls at an English boarding school, history abounding with kings thirty feet high and reigns thirty thousand years long, and geography made of seas of treacle and seas of butter.[93]

Macaulay, thus, did not think that the EIC ought to patronize Sanskrit and Arabic learning just because of its sanctity in the eyes of Indians. As he saw it, these classical languages were simply not worthy from the point of view of academics:

> It is said that Sanscrit [sic] and Arabic are the languages in which the sacred books of a hundred millions of people are written.... But to encourage the study of a literature ... of small intrinsic value ... is a course hardly reconcilable with reason.[94]

Because of his contempt for Indian languages and classical Oriental learning, we are tempted to imagine that Macaulay might have found the dispute between the Orientalists and the Anglicists quite pointless and without a genuine basis. As someone who considered 'a single shelf of a good European library ... worth the whole native literature of India and Arabia',[95] he very likely did not see anything moot about the latter's position and supported it from the very outset. Manifestly eager to set right the mistake that the EIC had committed in supporting Oriental learning, Macaulay pointed out that the Charter Act of 1813 did not bind it to a particular education policy and recommended that it promote English-medium education:

> I think it is clear that we are not fettered by the Act of Parliament of 1813 ... that we are free to employ our funds as we choose, that we ought to employ them in teaching what is best worth knowing, that is English is better worth knowing than Sanscrit [sic] or Arabic.

The head of the General Committee of Public Instruction also expressed an earnest wish to eradicate the setups until then patronized by the EIC in which Sanskrit and Arabic learning was imparted. As Macaulay put it in the minute, if he had his way, he 'would strike at the root of the bad system which has hitherto been fostered by us … [and] abolish the Mudrassa [sic] and the Sanscrit College at Calcutta'.[96]

'Macaulay's minute' was endorsed by the Governor-General, Lord William Bentinck, with remarkable alacrity. This was probably due to the utilitarian influence on his thinking.[97] Utilitarianism being a practical, broadly anti-tradition philosophy (a variant of liberal thought, it sought to abolish every usage purportedly without the 'utility' of promoting general happiness), it is very possible that Bentinck did not perceive any great value in the classical Sanskrit and Arabic learning the EIC had been supporting. Furthermore, Bentinck and Macaulay could both be seen as agents of a metropole eager to recast the colony in its own image. Macaulay, as it is, wanted to breed a class of 'persons Indian in blood and colour, but English in tastes, in opinions, in morals and in intellect'.[98] This high-level colonial administrator, in other words, wanted to impart the overall worldview and psychology of his compatriots to the natives. This project, of course, as we understand it, had its relevance to the efficient colonial exploitation of India in the capitalist mode. One, thus, cannot help but think that Bentinck and Macaulay, philosophical outlook and supremacist mindset apart, could be seeking to facilitate a certain political economy in the way of the colonial relationship between Great Britain and India.

A mere month after Macaulay penned his minute, on 7 March 1835, the Governor-General's Council passed a resolution:

> [T]he great object of the British Government ought to be the promotion of European literature and science among the natives of India; and that all the funds appropriated for the purpose of education would be best employed on English education alone.[99]

The EIC regime, in other words, unambiguously committed itself to the furtherance of English-medium Western education in India and made a clean break with the education policy it had followed until then. However, all the institutions of Oriental learning were not wound up immediately as Macaulay had wished. But the resolution decided not to make any new faculty appointments therein as replacements for the retirees. It also declared that the forthcoming batches of students in these institutions shall not be paid a stipend. The Oriental institutions of learning, thus, were downsized in terms of teaching staff and, as it seems, considerably deprived of funds. The 'large sum' that was earlier 'expended' by the General Committee of Public Instruction on the publication of 'Oriental works' was completely discontinued by this resolution. It mandated that no funds 'shall hereafter be so employed'.[100] This was indeed a very comprehensive policy U-turn on the part of the EIC.

The Orientalists, however, did not give up and continued their controversy with the Anglicists. But it was to no avail, and Lord Auckland (1784–1839), one of Bentinck's successors, ensured that the policy reversal was for good.[101]

The Orientalist education policy of the EIC, thus, met its demise. However, as far as we see, the Company did not immediately seek to promote English-medium Western education through some major initiative in mass instruction. The EIC's administration, instead, based its system of education on the 'downward filtration theory'[102] after 1835. That is, its chief focus remained the institutions of higher learning and the education of small numbers of elite Indians therein. The Company hoped that education would percolate downwards into Indian society with these upper-class Indians teaching their compatriots from the lower social strata. As before, resultantly, the EIC undertook no serious effort to establish its own network of schools across its territories. Munro's plan in this regard, as we know, was abandoned after some perfunctory work. Worse, the indigenous Indian schools were neglected (in the Bombay[103] and Madras Presidencies,[104] for instance) and neither active assistance (in the form of funds) nor encouragement of any kind was provided to them. Once again, it appears, the chief non-Indian agency active in the field of mass instruction in the aftermath of the EIC's revision of its education policy were the Christian missionaries. In the Madras Presidency, as we learn, they conducted their activities 'on a very large scale', and imparted English education.[105]

The Charter Act of 1833, as a matter of fact, had caused a spurt in missionary activity in the EIC's Indian territories by throwing them open to the representatives of churches from outside Great Britain. Several German and American missions availed of the opportunity to begin their work in British-ruled India. The Bassel Mission Society, the Protestant Lutheran Missionary Society, and the Women's

Association of Education of Females in the Orient are some instances of the former. A few American missions that arrived in India, on the other hand, were the American Baptists, the American Board, the Presbyterians, and the Church Missionary Society.[106]

Largely, at this juncture, the missionaries seem to have enjoyed cordial relations with the EIC's administration (if not its active support). This was partly due to the 'missionary zeal' of many officials, and partly the abandonment of the earlier policy of religious neutrality, on the part of the EIC regime; it had lost its old hesitancy about offending Hindu and Muslim religious sensibilities.[107] Apparently, the Company men were also friendly towards the missionaries in their educational work on account of the situation back home. Mass instruction in England was still provided by the various denominational schools as an act of charity with grants-in-aid from the government. The EIC's officials, thus, thought that the education of the masses in India could be similarly left to missionary charity.[108]

The last major policy statement regarding education by the EIC regime, before it was swept away by the great uprising of 1857, was in the form of the 'Wood's despatch'. This was a lengthy document of one hundred paragraphs authored by Charles Wood, the President of the EIC's Board of Control,[109] in 1854. The first two paragraphs of the text illustrated the motivations behind the EIC undertaking the education of Indians, rendering them fit to discharge administrative offices and instilling in them the beneficial industriousness of the metropole, so that they subserve its economic interests by supplying its manufacturing with raw materials and generously consuming its output:

> We have … always looked upon the encouragement of education as peculiarly important, … not only to produce a higher degree of intellectual fitness, but to raise the moral character of those who partake of its advantages, and … supply … servants to whose probity … [the Governor-General] may with increased confidence commit offices of trust … in India…
>
> Nor, … [are England's] material interests altogether unaffected by the advance of … knowledge in India; … [it] will teach the natives of India the marvelous results of the employment of labour and capital, rouse them to emulate us in the development of the vast resources of their country … confer upon them all the advantages which accompany the healthy increase of wealth and commerce; and … secure to us a larger and more certain supply of many articles necessary for our manufactures … as well as an almost inexhaustible demand for the produce of British labour.[110]

The despatch, in other words, very candidly confessed to the political economy of, as we shall term it today, 'coloniality', that is, the broad framework of capitalist exploitation that had come to underlie the acculturation of Indians undertaken by the EIC (which was, by now, less of the mercantile firm it once was and more of, so to speak, an administrative agency holding its Indian territories in trust for Great Britain). The document also provided a pragmatic plan to advance this acculturation, namely, the instruction of Indians in Western knowledge:

> [T]he education that we desire to see extended in India … [is the] science, philosophy and literature of Europe; in short … Western knowledge…

> We have to consider the manner in which our object is to be effected…
>
> In any general system of education, the English language should be taught where there is a demand for it; but such instruction should always be combined with a careful attention to the study of the vernacular language of the district … the vernacular languages must be employed to teach the far larger classes who are ignorant of, or imperfectly acquainted with English. This can be done effectually through the instrumentality of masters and professors, who may, by themselves, knowing English and thus having full access to the latest improvements in knowledge of every kind, impart to their fellow countrymen through the medium of their mother tongue, the information which they have thus obtained…
>
> We look, therefore, to the English language and to the vernacular languages of India together as the *media* for the diffusion of European knowledge, and it is our desire to see them cultivated together in all schools in India of a sufficiently high class to maintain a school-master possessing the requisite qualifications.[111] (Italics in original)

In short, Wood thought that Western education need not be imparted in India in the English medium alone. Instead, he proposed that this is done through a strategic balance between English and the Indian languages by employing teachers equally conversant in both. They would teach English where the knowledge of the language was much sought. Otherwise, they would use their own knowledge of English to access Western knowledge and subsequently convey it to their pupils in the local tongue.

After dwelling on the matter of the medium of instruction for Indian pupils, the despatch took a couple of vital decisions regarding the overall administrative framework for education in the EIC's territories. It created a Department of Public Instruction for the three Presidencies (Bengal, Madras, and Bombay), as well as the North-Western Province (present day Uttar Pradesh) and Punjab under the Director of Public Instruction. Wood also took the momentous decision of establishing a university in each of the three Presidency capitals. Consequently, the Universities of Calcutta, Madras, and Bombay were founded in 1857. These were modelled after the University of London, with their senates comprising a Chancellor, Vice-Chancellor, and Fellows, all nominated by the government. Last but not the least, Wood visualized an educational system organized as a graded, pyramidal network of institutions, with the universities in the coastal Presidencies at the top, followed by the English or vernacular (Indian language) medium high schools, and the indigenous schools forming the foundation.[112] The gentleman, it seems, was keen to give an impetus to school-level education by encouraging private initiative. To this end, Wood recommended a system of grants-in-aid for private schools if they met certain criteria: teaching a secular curriculum, 'a good local management', being amenable to regular inspection, and levying 'a fee, however small, from the pupils'.[113] Wood, it seems, was keen about advancing mass instruction and his despatch, thus, was a departure from the 'downward filtration theory'.

Indian Education in the Remainder of the 19th Century

'Wood's depatch' settled the colonial educational system in terms of the essentials: Western curriculum, English and the Indian languages both (depending on practicability) serving as mediums of instruction, a Department of Public Instruction run by the Director of Public Instruction, a university system on top of a tiered network of schools, and, finally, a system of grants-in-aid as support to private initiative in schooling. With these basics in place, the chief shifts or changes in the education scene in the remainder of the 19th century were in missionary activity, the level of government involvement, the scope of Indian initiative, and indigenous schooling.

Christian missionaries, by far, were the most active agency in Indian education in 1854, when Wood wrote his despatch. However, in the latter half of the 1800s there was a noticeable decline in their activity. First, this was because they were unable to use the Western education they provided as successfully as an instrument of proselytization as they had initially hoped. Missionary educational initiatives were, thus, thwarted by the low yield of converts. Second, the colonial administration, after the inception of Crown rule in India in 1858, ceased to be friendly towards the missionaries and adopted a policy of religious neutrality.[114] This was done to ensure that the religious sensibilities of Indians are not offended and there is no repeat of the uprising of 1857.

As a corollary to the colonial administration's policy of not encouraging the missionaries, the Department of Education, as far as possible, from 1858 to 1882, sought to run schools and colleges under its direct supervision.[115] There was, in this way, a progressive intensification of the government's involvement in education. The trend was somewhat reversed by the Indian Education Commission. Appointed in 1882, it recommended that the government transfer the primary schools it was running to the municipalities and local boards, and the secondary schools and colleges to the private agencies. Subsequently, until 1902, the government did entrust the primary schools to the local bodies. However, this did not mean a withdrawal of the government from primary education in substantive terms and its transfer to elected Indian representatives (local self-government was introduced in 1883), since these bodies were dominated by the 'official element',[116] that is, the bureaucrats. The secondary and collegiate educational institutions were, on the other hand, largely not transferred to the local bodies.[117] However, the colonial administration adopted the course of encouraging private initiative in secondary and collegiate education.[118]

Since the government was now wary of the missionaries, Indian activity received a major boost in this area. Especially since, in this period, there were major social and religious reform efforts underway in Indian society which, mostly, adopted education as one of the means to achieve their objectives. Higher education was especially an area in which Indians were interested. In fact, Indian initiative in higher education expanded so rapidly between 1882 and 1901–02 that the missionaries, once the leading private agency in the field, were put behind. As we observe, in 1901–02, there were forty-two colleges under Indian management, compared to thirty-seven under missionary management.[119] Concomitant to the major growth of Indian initiative in higher education, ironically, was the near complete extinction of indigenous schooling. This was mainly due to two reasons: the want of support from the colonial state and the disappearance of the system of revenue allotments (by the old, landed elites) that had previously been its foremost source of sustenance.[120]

The backdrop to Pandit Madan Mohan Malviya's activism for a Hindu institution of higher learning, thus, was a colonial education scene characterized by the incontrovertible hegemony of Western curriculum, retreat of missionary effort and government involvement, a significant expansion of Indian initiative, and the perishing of the 'beautiful tree' of indigenous education. From Malaviya's perspective, this might have looked like a situation requiring redress and yet replete with opportunities. The visionary that he was, he realized that the current colonial education policy could be leveraged for a uniquely Indian and Hindu intervention in higher academia. Very astutely, Malaviya formulated this intervention in a way that it would represent the intellectual heritage of the land and yet fit into the Western curriculum-based framework of contemporary higher education. He was a Hindu educationist with a remarkable catholicity of outlook and intellect.

2

Madan Mohan Malaviya: A Hindu Educationist

A Confluence of Worlds

Madan Mohan Malaviya was born in Allahabad (now Prayagraj) on 25 December 1861 into a devout and scholarly Brahmin family. The Malaviyas had migrated to what were then the North-Western Provinces and Oudh (NWP&O, now Uttar Pradesh) from the Malwa region of central India in the 15th century. This was, as we learn, on account of an insult meted to their Pancha Gauda subcaste by the local Raja.[1] Due to their origins in Malwa, they initially came to be called 'Mallai' and, in due course, 'Malaviya.'[2]

Malaviya's father, Pandit Brij Nath, possessed remarkable traditional erudition, even by the high standards of his illustrious lineage. He, it is said, acquired felicity and fame as an expositor of the Bhagavata at a very young age.[3] Brij Nath was, consequently, bestowed with the title of 'Vyasa' while only twenty-five,[4] it indicated his expertise in relating the sacred lore. Besides the Bhagavata, Brij Nath was also known for his recitations of the Ramayana, all of which he had committed to the memory.[5] Wedded to the pious and accomplished

Moona Devi, Brij Nath begot six sons and two daughters. Malaviya was the fifth among them.

Malaviya received his early lessons at home in Sanskrit from his learned father. His formal schooling was at multiple institutions. He attended the Shri Dharma Gyanopdesh Pathshala for a few years where Brahmanical orthopraxis such as the application of the tilak (the sacred marking on the forehead) and the timely performance of sandhya (the evening prayers) were strictly inculcated. Later, Malaviya moved to the Vidyadharma Pravardhani Pathshala. The head of the institution, Pandit Deokinandan, it seems, was quite fond of him. This was probably because Malaviya had inherited his father's talent for giving religious discourses. Deokinandan, thus, would accompany the precocious lad to the annual Magh Mela, when thousands of pilgrims gathered at the confluence of the Ganga and the Yamuna for a purificatory ritual bath, 'and ask him to speak from some pulpit at a street crossing'.[6]

At the two pathshalas, apparent vestiges of indigenous schooling, lessons were imparted in Sanskrit and Hindi. However, Malaviya dearly wanted to attend an English-medium school.[7] The eager learner that he was, he might have been keen to acquire the English language. Despite his modest means as a preacher and expounder of sacred texts, his father kept his wish and enrolled him in the Allahabad District School. Malaviya remained there until his matriculation.

Malaviya joined Muir Central College after his matriculation. He earned a BA from there in 1884 (with History, English, and Sanskrit). Thereafter, he embarked on an MA in Sanskrit. Unfortunately, Malaviya had to drop out of his postgraduate studies due to the straitened circumstances at home[8] and begin earning a livelihood as a schoolmaster. Although abruptly curtailed, the stint at the Muir Central College, we are told, 'proved very fruitful and momentous in the full development of [Malaviya's] personality and talents.'[9]

Malaviya mingled freely at college, not allowing himself to be constrained by inherited social prejudices or orthodoxies as a high-born Brahmin. His friends, thus, came from every social stratum in terms of their jati identities. Further, Malaviya encountered Mahamahopadhyaya Aditya Ram Bhattacharya, at Muir Central College. This professor of Sanskrit was an extremely altruistic human being. He made a profound impression on the young Malaviya and instilled in him a spirit of public service. The principal of the institution, Professor H. Harrison, was also a major influence on Malaviya.[10] Looking up to the English gentleman, we imagine, Malaviya might have been drawn towards the Western learning he represented. While at Muir Central College, Malaviya also began contributing on public issues to periodicals such as *Hindi Pradip* and *Indian Union.*[11] He in other words, developed into a socially broad-minded, altruistic, and intellectually keen youth at college.

Malaviya enrolled in the LLB programme at Allahabad University after a few years as a working professional (he quit his teaching job in 1887 to take up the editorship of a newspaper). Apparently, he was motivated to do so by none other than A.O. Hume (1829–1912), whom he met at the second annual session of the Indian National Congress in 1886. Hume, it seems, wanted this bright young man to earn a legal education so that he could deploy it in public good. Malaviya received his law degree in 1892.

While an LLB student, we learn, Malaviya 'took a special interest in constitutional law, pertaining to rights of the subjects to refuse to obey the arbitrary orders of a magistrate'.[12] Maybe, this was because the nationalist in him wanted to help his fellow Indians tackle the pitfalls of colonial legal administration. After being called to the bar, Malaviya began his legal career at the Allahabad District Court. He would later move to the provincial High Court.

Malaviya was a remarkably conscientious lawyer. He accepted only as many cases as 'he could ordinarily accommodate and insisted on his clients being honest'. He was also a very competent lawyer with a 'rare power of eloquence'.[13] In time, Malaviya grew to be a very successful legal professional earning 'thousands of rupees per month',[14] a veritable fortune in those days. Eventually, however, he quit this lucrative legal career to chiefly devote his time and energy to the goal of establishing a Hindu institution of higher education.

Malaviya's intellect and personality were a confluence of worlds, where the best of Indian and Western learning mingled. Due to his family background and early education, he was every bit the learned Hindu pandit. But he also received the finest liberal arts education available in colonial India. Malaviya, in this way, was the cultivated Victorian gentleman too. He, thus, always displayed a remarkable catholicity of outlook and conduct in public life. Malaviya subscribed to basic liberal values in his politics, and yet remained the traditional Hindu. He was a man bereft of rigidities and dogmas, a mean between opposites and extremes.

Malaviya in Public Life: Congressman and Hindu Activist

Malaviya's relationship with the Indian National Congress (henceforth only Congress) began when the organization was just a year old, while he himself was a green youth of twenty-five. As it turned out, he would be associated with this premier political forum in British-ruled India for half a century and serve as its president four times (in 1909, 1918, 1932, and 1933). Malaviya, therefore, was something of a dyed-in-the-wool Congressman. He retired from the party only when he grew too old and infirm to continue participating in its activities.

As a Congressman, Malaviya was a liberal constitutionalist, or 'moderate', who first strove to secure political representation for Indians (along with others of his kind) and then used the colonial representative bodies to articulately advance an Indian point of view on public affairs. Speaking at the annual session of the Congress in 1886 (conducted in Calcutta), the first he attended, Malaviya forcefully sought representative bodies for his country. Betraying a youthful energy, he jumped up on a chair[15] and pointed out to the colonial authorities that they came from an innately democratic society and urged them to live up to its values:

> What is an Englishman without representative institutions? … I often wonder as I look around at our nominally English magnates how they have the face to call themselves Englishmen and yet deny us representative institutions and struggle to maintain despotic ones. Representative institutions are as much a part of the true Briton as his language and literature…. No taxation without representation. That is the first commandment in the Englishman's Political Bible; how can he palter with his

> conscience and tax us here, his free and educated fellow-subjects, as if we were dumb sheep or cattle?[16]

The much-appreciated speech at the second annual Congress—Hume would later recall that it 'carried everyone before him'[17]—was by no means a one-off performance by Malaviya. He would go on demanding representative bodies for India as forcefully and eloquently for many subsequent years from the Congress platform. In 1887, for instance, when the Congress assembled in Madras for its yearly session, Malaviya argued that the entire 'civilized world' had acknowledged that 'the wants and wishes, and aspirations and grievances of the people can be adequately set forth, properly understood or duly provided for' only through representative bodies. He, consequently, termed them 'essential, for the well-being of the country' and demanded that they are 'conceded' to India 'without the least avoidable delay'.[18]

Malaviya dwelt on the Indians' right to political representation yet again in 1889, when the Congress conducted its annual session in Bombay. As on previous occasions, his tone was impassioned and rhetorical:

> [W]e should no longer be debarred from exercising this simple and rightful privilege [of electing representatives to the Legislative Councils]. The privilege of selecting one's own counsel is not denied even to the most abandoned of criminals under the British rule. Why then should it be denied to the loyal and intelligent subjects of Her Gracious Majesty?[19]

Finding the Queen unresponsive towards her worthy Indian subjects, it seems, Malaviya yet again appealed to the putative democratic values of the English people in 1891. Addressing the annual meeting of the Congress at Nagpur, Malaviya termed, rather remarkably, Indians and the English kindreds, and entreated the latter to bestow the benefits of their own usages upon the former. Only in the likelihood of them doing so, he declared, would India redound to Britain's prestige as a political possession:

> We appeal to the English people who are our brethren to make the administration of this country more in conformity with reason, with justice, and with common sense, with those high and noble principles which have always been their pride, and which have raised them to the proud position which they now occupy before the world. Then and then alone, will British rule in India be the glory, as it should be, of England.[20]

The near obsequiousness exhibited by Malaviya towards the British Crown, along with his seemingly wide-eyed admiration for English institutions and usages is liable to make us uneasy today. Him terming Indians and the English brother peoples is even likely to make a few of us cringe, for, as far as rhetoric goes, it sounds rather mawkish and even callous. One wonders if Malaviya was ignorant of the depredations that the English had wreaked in India, or he simply did not care about them. Malaviya's pronouncements, however, need to be read in their proper historical context.

To begin with, Malaviya and his ilk in the Congress were acutely aware of the might of Great Britain as an imperial power. The unqualified ruthlessness with which the British had crushed the uprising of 1857 was still vividly remembered in the part of India Malaviya came from. He, thus, it is very likely, was being more tactful than sincere while adopting a supplicatory tone towards the British sovereign. The fulsome admiration he expressed for, as he thought, an inherently democratic Great Britain (where, ironically, only propertied males exercised the franchise at the time) may be termed some naivete. It might be, one surmises, on account of an idealized image of that country that he had received through college education.

Malaviya's academic background had turned him into, as we called him above, something of a Victorian gentleman. He was, resultantly, filled with an instinctive admiration (in certain matters) for the metropole and its history, culture, and institutions. In this regard, Malaviya was no different from the common run of Congressmen in those days. The 19th-century Congress was largely composed of Western-educated professional elites who looked up to Great Britain. Significantly, this caused them to repose faith in the metropole's ostensible sense of justice and fair play and imagine that both the English and Indians are equal imperial subjects in the eyes of its sovereign. Malaviya effusively called the two 'brethren' because, very likely, he shared in this misplaced faith and imagination (it is worth noting that he had called Indians the 'free and educated fellow-subjects' of the English during his maiden speech as a Congressman). The young Malaviya, in this way, was but voicing the dominant point of view in the Congress.

Malaviya's seeming deference towards the British Crown and his fraternal and admiring attitude towards the English people, thus, derived from a specific historical situation and its determinants. He, one must know, was never aligned with the colonial administration. Malaviya criticized it at every opportune turn to secure his country a better and fairer treatment. He was always acutely aware of the plight of Indians under British rule.

After representative bodies (with very limited powers) were finally conceded to India at the provinces and centre, Malaviya served stints in the United Provinces (as the NWP&O was renamed in 1902) Legislative Council (from 1902 to 1912) and the Imperial Legislative Council (from 1912 to 1919 and 1923 to 1930). At both forums, he never flinched from pointing out the ills and failings of the colonial administration and attempted to sensitize it towards Indians' woes. For instance, in 1904, Malaviya dwelt in the UP Legislative Council on the chronic indebtedness among cultivators in the Bundelkhand region due to the colonial land revenue system's 'rigidity' and tendency for 'over-assessment'.[21] He, subsequently, introduced an amendment to the 'Bundelkhand Encumbered Estates Bill' that was under discussion in the house to keep a creditor from auctioning off a cultivator's 'dwelling-house' to 'realize his debt'.[22]

Malaviya was both sincere and voluble as a provincial legislator. He, as we see, was present in fifteen out of the seventeen sittings of the UP Legislative Council from 1904 to 1909. His speeches cover 'one-sixth of the total proceedings' of the house in this period. This is even more significant when one learns that on an average the body met for only two and a half days in a year. Malaviya, in this way, 'made the most of the limited opportunities' that its membership brought him for 'scrutinizing the functions of the provincial administration'.[23]

Besides, as we have seen, focusing on issues concerning agriculture, Malaviya tellingly reflected on industry, education, public health, and local self-government[24] from an Indian perspective in the UP Legislative Council. As a provincial legislator, Malaviya worked to ensure that the United Provinces' administration responded to the 'demands of the people'.[25] He, in other words, tried to make it less of a bureaucratic autocracy and more accountable, being deeply committed to the ideal of responsible government.

Malaviya continued his efforts to make the colonial administration responsible and aligned with the ideals of the representative system in the Imperial Legislative Council.[26] When the repressive 'Press Bill' aimed at stopping the dissemination of 'seditious' literature, was tabled in the house in 1910, Malaviya opposed it vehemently. He expressed concern about the fact that, like the Vernacular Press Act of 1878, the bill intended to take the power of determining what writing is seditious out of the hands of 'established legal jurisdiction' and place it in those of the government.[27] Malaviya urged the government not to add 'one more repressive measure on the Statute Book'.[28] Furthermore, he argued that the bill might constrain the newspapers to 'write under a greater sense of restraint than is needed for the purposes of good administration' and (unsuccessfully) demanded that it is no more considered by the house.[29] Malaviya, in other words, stood up for the Indian press's right to criticize the regime and seek general welfare from it.

He also used his membership of the Imperial Legislative Council to plead the case for greater decentralization. Malaviya's objective behind this was to ensure that public welfare is more efficiently served. When the budget came up for discussion in the house in 1910, Malaviya stressed the need for a better financial arrangement between central and provincial governments 'so that the latter could spend more on public works'.[30] Rationalizing and, if possible, curtailing governmental expenses were constant focus areas for him in the Imperial Legislative Council. In the years that he sat in the house, Malaviya passed resolutions to effect 'reduction on the expense of various departments, such as stationery and printing, railways, mint, salt, police, and so on'.[31] Apparently, his intention was to make greater sums available for welfare works. He also used his membership of the Imperial Legislative Council to decry and redress blatant colonial oppression. In 1916, for example, he moved a bill in the house demanding the abolition of the indentured labour system. It involved the recruitment of Indians (often through fraud) to work in sugarcane, banana, or tobacco plantations in far off British colonies in near slavery conditions; the hours of work would be inhumanly long and the wages a mere pittance. Mincing no words, Malaviya termed indentured labour 'thoroughly indefensible' and declared:

> [N]o reforms will prove sufficient; tinkering will not do; the system must be abolished root and branch … Nothing short of a complete abolition of the system [will do] … and it is the duty of the Government of India to take that step unhesitatingly.[32]

Malaviya, as it ought to be apparent by now, was something of a classical liberal. He believed that government should be responsible, oriented towards general welfare and happiness, subject to legitimate criticism (hence his opposition to the Press Bill), and ultimately just and humane.

Malaviya strove to achieve this form of government in British ruled India in a chiefly constitutionalist paradigm of action. He, in other words, worked in the frameworks of political representation and legislative procedures granted by the colonial administration to realize his objective. Malaviya, one might say, attempted to make the best of these frameworks for his country, just as, as a lawyer, he sought to make the best of the interstices of the colonial legal system for his clients.

Due to his fundamentally liberal constitutionalist outlook, Malaviya nurtured a certain unease towards agitational politics. This was probably because it inevitably involved aggressive and, sometimes, dogmatic posturing. A person of his bent of mind could not be comfortable with that. Nevertheless, Malaviya would still go out of his way to stand up for a political agitator if they were being unduly victimized by the colonial regime. For instance, when Annie Besant launched her Home Rule League in 1916, he initially preferred to keep aloof. However, he was quick to lend her support when the colonial authorities bore down on the initiative and sought to stamp it out.

On 18 June 1917, Malaviya wrote a letter to the editor of the *Leader* newspaper and praised the 'splendid manner in which … [Annie Besant was] sacrificing herself at her age in the cause of India's progress and reform'. He expressed the hope that 'she … [would] be allowed to go on with her work'.[33] Later, after Besant was interned by the Madras Presidency administration, Malaviya tabled a resolution in the Imperial Legislative Council demanding her early release. He also toured multiple cities meeting with regional and local politicians and impressed upon them the 'gross injustice' meted out to Besant.[34] Then, on

8 August 1917, Malaviya addressed a 'mammoth public meeting under the auspices of the Home Rule League'.[35] On this occasion, it seems, he acknowledged his compatriots' right to resort to agitational politics in principle, even if he himself was not a part of it. As the Chief Secretary of the United Provinces later reported, Malaviya observed that the 'mistake of Indians had been not to agitate sufficiently'[36] during his speech.

Thus, even if a certain mode of politics contrasted with his own, he would come around to it if convinced of its justice. Malaviya did not perceive the world in terms of rigid, non-negotiable binaries. He always considered the *purva paksha*, the other point of view, and, it appears, heeded it if prompted by reason and his ethical sense. Malaviya was, in this way, once again a liberal, and we shall aver, deeply Hindu. Just like the Home Rule League, for instance, he had initial misgivings about the Gandhian Civil Disobedience Movement. Malaviya was not quite in agreement with the 'Purna Swaraj' resolution, passed at the 1929 annual session of the Congress in Lahore, in whose pursuance it was launched. Nevertheless, he still eventually participated in the Civil Disobedience Movement and courted arrest.[37] Malaviya would later highlight the plight of those jailed in it in a lengthy public statement. As the following excerpt shows, it was a scathing indictment of the colonial administration:

> In these hot months they [the prisoners] are huddled up inside barracks ... covered merely with corrugated iron sheets which convert the barracks into something like the neighborhood of an oven. Yet, there have been cases where sufficient water was not given them to drink during the

> day. Boys have been flogged inside jails merely for shouting Vande Mataram or for other petty offences. In some places for want of accommodation C class political prisoners are left in the open inside jails and they are secured by an iron chain being passed through iron rings which are put on one of their legs and riveted so that they cannot be taken out until they are cut … But the worst treatment has been given to the women prisoners. They are ill-treated and harassed. In one case, a group of twelve of them in a lock up was severely beaten with lathis, kicks and fists and some of them were stripped naked.[38]

Malaviya, as we see, was as diligent and outspoken a political agitator as he was a legislator. Like any liberal, and, in our view, Hindu, Malaviya was a believer in dialogue. For instance, if not for the dialogue he facilitated between the 'moderates' and 'extremists' in the Congress, they might have fallen out much before 1907.[39] He also sought to facilitate dialogue between Gandhi and the Viceroy during the Non-Cooperation Movement[40] (which he kept away from, disagreeing with its programme). Again, after Malaviya joined the Swaraj Party (established in 1923 by Motilal Nehru and C.R. Das), he played interlocutor between its two factions: the 'responsivists' and the 'non-responsivists'. The former, whom Malaviya sympathized with, wanted to use the legislative councils to expedite the attainment of Swaraj. Also, they did not mind accepting political office. The non-responsivists, on the other hand, planned to enter the colonial representative bodies only to wreck them.

When nothing came out of his efforts of forging an agreement between the two camps, Malaviya formed the

Independent Congress Party (ICP) in 1926 with Lala Lajpat Rai (1865–1928), M.R. Jayakar (1873–1959), B.S. Moonje (1872–1948), and N.C. Kelkar (1872–1947). One of its objectives was to work the legislative bodies 'to the best possible advantage'.[41] The ICP, as we understand, positioned itself in between the responsivists and the non-responsivists (despite Malaviya's inclination for the former). It neither planned to cooperate with the government through representative bodies, nor sought to destroy them from the inside. This pragmatic reasonableness and eschewal of extreme positions on the part of the ICP, we imagine, was probably on account of Malaviya. After considering two contrary outlooks, he had found, as a liberal and a Hindu, an intermediary position between them. This capacity was quite characteristic of Malaviya, and, as we shall see, he also brought it to his views as an educationist.

Malaviya was a very capable publicist in the colonial public sphere. Impressed by his oratorial performance at the second annual Congress, Raja Ram Pal Singh (1849–1909) of the Kalakankar Estate, a delegate in attendance, offered him the editorship of the daily owned by him. It was called *The Hindustan.* Malaviya took up the role in 1887 and discharged it competently. The government of the NWP&O termed it the best-edited Indian newspaper in its annual report for 1888–89. Politically, *The Hindustan* stood with the Congress. It was also into cultural advocacy. Malaviya used the daily to promote the cause of the Hindi language.[42] At that time, Hindi rendered in the Devanagari script had emerged as a core cultural symbol for Hindus in colonial North India. A Hindu mobilization of sorts, consequently, strove to secure official recognition for it. Chiefly, the Hindi–Nagari agitation, as it is called today, sought to end Urdu's status as the sole language of the colonial legal administration in the NWP&O, Bihar, and the Central Provinces. It demanded that court proceedings be also recorded, along with Urdu, in Hindi and the Devanagari script.

Malaviya emerged as a prominent Hindu activist in the colonial public sphere by enthusiastically championing the administrative reform sought by the Hindi–Nagari agitators. He was associated with the Nagri Pracharni Sabha, an organization at the forefront of the Hindi–Nagari agitation, from its inception at Banaras in 1893.[43] Then, in 1897, Malaviya authored an extremely well-researched tract, 'Court Character and Primary Education in the N.-W. Provinces & Oudh', to persuade colonial authorities to make Hindi the concomitant language of legal administration. To begin with, it argued that 'Hindi was the vernacular language of Hindustan' at the time of the arrival of the 'Muhammadans' and 'all business was carried on' then in the 'Nagri character, or its variations'.[44] Malaviya, thus, tried to establish that the formal use of Hindi and the Devanagari script is not without historical precedent, and it is the authentic pre-Islamic heritage of the land. He also contested Urdu's status as an independent language, terming it the argot of a specific social group. Malaviya also argued that the preponderate population of the Hindi-speaking regions of British-ruled India (that is, the Hindus) finds this argot exotic and difficult to understand:

> The Persianized dialect of Hindi, known as Urdu … chiefly in use among educated Musalmans and amlas connected with courts … [is] by reason of preponderance of Persian, Arabic and Turkish words, and the fact of its being written

> in Persian characters, practically foreign and unintelligible to the vast majority of the people in these Provinces [NWP&O, Bihar, and the Central Provinces].[45]

Malaviya, in other words, tried to impress upon the colonial authorities that the exclusive use of Urdu in legal administration made scant practical sense in regions where the population was preponderantly Hindu and Hindi-speaking. It simply made the legal process too arcane for them. The inconsistencies and hard to read nature of the Persian script, in which Urdu was rendered, Malaviya thought, compounded this problem:

> [T]he inherent defects of the Persian characters and the extreme illegibility of Persian writing as it is ordinarily written, make them entirely unsuitable for the purposes of the proceedings of courts and public offices in this country.[46]

Besides hindering the transparency of the legal process for the Hindus and Hindi speakers, Malaviya pointed out, the Persian script made it liable to criminal manipulation:

> [T]his faulty system of writing lends itself readily to the purposes of fabrication, as alterations can be made in it by the addition of a merest stroke or dot here and there which the utmost skill of a court of justice would not unoften fail to detect.[47]

Malaviya argued that the Devanagari characters are both more legible and systematic[48] and in 'far greater use' in the NWP&O, Bihar, and the Central Provinces than the Persian ones.[49] He, thus, pointed out to the colonial authorities 'the justice, expediency, and necessity of substituting the Nagri character for Persian in the courts of these Provinces'.[50] Besides streamlining the legal administration, in Malaviya's view, this was also required for the advancement of education in the NWP&O, Bihar, and the Central Provinces. He thought that their majority population fared poorly in education because it was compelled to seek it in a language which was not its own, namely Urdu, just because it was privileged by the rulers. He, thus, forcefully argued:

> So long as Urdu, surcharged with difficult Persian and Arabic words and written in Persian characters, occupies the position of the sole officially-recognized vernacular in these Provinces ... the progress of education and civilization ... [in them] will remain hopefully obstructed.[51]

The Hindi–Nagari agitation bore fruit in the NWP&O not long after Malaviya penned the foregoing. In 1900, after a spell of consultations, the Lieutenant-Governor of the Province, Sir Antony MacDonnell (1844–1925), gave the Hindi language and the Devanagari script a status equivalent to Urdu 'in certain areas of official business'.[52] Along with the popular mobilization and press campaign in their favour, we imagine, a factor at work behind the decision might have been Malaviya's consummately argued tract.

Malaviya had been oriented towards Hindu activism, or an association with causes concerning the dignity and overall welfare of Hindu society, by Aditya Ram Bhattacharya. He, it seems, motivated Malaviya to join the 'newly established' Hindu Samaj in Allahabad. The organization worked for the 'uplift of Hindus' and to advance Hindu interests. Its members also rendered volunteer service at the annual Magh Mela.[53] Malaviya very actively took part in its endeavours. Later, the Hindu Samaj became a provincial level organization and renamed itself the Madhya Hindu Samaj. It also became one of the many organizations accredited by the Congress to send delegates to its annual sessions.[54] Malaviya, thus, began his career in the Congress (when he spoke at its second annual session) as a representative of the Madhya Hindu Samaj. He, as we see, became a Congressman by way of Hindu activism.

Along with Hindi–Nagari, the cow was another core cultural symbol around which Hindus rallied in large numbers in colonial North India. The phenomenon was especially intense in the NWP&O, where Malaviya came from. As Sandria Freitag observes, between 1888 and 1890, efforts at preventing cow slaughter were organized on such a large scale in the province that they 'swept … [its] urban centers'.[55] Being a devout Hindu, Malaviya of course strongly identified with the cause of cow protection. He also took a rational, economic view of the issue. Malviya looked at it from the point of view of national health as well. Preventing cow slaughter was a necessity, he believed, because the animal was essential to the agricultural economy. Its slaughter, he argued, would make bullocks scarce and, resultantly, Indian agriculture would suffer. Further, Malaviya feared that cow slaughter would cause the scarcity of milk[56] and make the population susceptible to diseases. He sought to advance the cause of cow protection peacefully by securing the cooperation of the beef-eating religious groups, viz., Muslims and Christians. Malaviya, thus, engaged in several 'unity talks' with Muslims to win their goodwill and dissuade them from cow slaughter. Finally, besides opposing cow slaughter on economic and health grounds, Malaviya took a moral objection to it. As he put it, 'The animal that gives us milk and butter should not be given to butchers because it … [has] ceased to give milk, in the same way as we do not discard our old mothers.'[57]

Malaviya veered towards the All-India Hindu Mahasabha (henceforth just Hindu Mahasabha) because, as we learn, he was unhappy with the bias shown by the colonial administration in favour of the Muslim community.[58] Also, he believed that Congress, on account of being a political organization, was not well placed to deal with community matters. Malaviya, consequently, felt the need for an organization that would speak on behalf of Hindus about the issues concerning them.[59] As we understand, the Hindu Mahasabha (founded in 1915 as the All-India Hindu Sabha, it was renamed in 1921), in his perception, was the answer to this need. Malaviya appeared on its platform for the first time in 1916, chiefly, it seems, to vent his frustration regarding the 'Lucknow Pact'. It was an agreement between Congress and All-India Muslim League under which the former had conceded 'weightage' to Muslims. Simply put, this meant that the Congress acknowledged Muslims' entitlement to political representation in excess of their numbers in Hindu-majority provinces. Subsequently, Malaviya addressed a meeting of the Hindu Mahasabha in Banaras in which he stressed that only justice and fair play could be the bases of communal harmony.[60]

After a few years of relatively desultory association, Malaviya drew closer to the Hindu Mahasabha in 1922, in the wake of the Multan riots, during which Hindus suffered grievously, and the massacre and forced conversion of Hindus perpetrated by the Muslim Moplah peasants in

Malabar (today's Kerala). He was elected the organization's president at its annual session in Gaya that year. During his address, he excoriated Hindus for their weakness and inability to defend themselves. While being Hindu naturally entailed respecting all religions, Malaviya affirmed, it also required one to defend oneself when attacked and, if it came to that, die in the process. He also suggested that Hindu Sabhas be formed in every village to work for 'Hindu unity and regeneration'. Further, Malaviya got the Hindu Mahasabha to pass a resolution urging Hindu leaders of Malabar to 'unhesitatingly' readmit into the Hindu fold all victims of forced conversions.[61]

Next year, when the Hindu Mahasabha met in Banaras for its annual session, Malaviya once again rued the Hindu inability for self-defense.[62] He also proposed reforms to reinvigorate Hindu society; promotion of women's education, the elimination of extremely early marriages, and curtailment of dowry demands.[63] The highlight of this annual session of the Hindu Mahasabha was the adoption of a resolution, chiefly due to the efforts of Malaviya, acknowledging the 'need for making arrangements' so that the 'untouchables' could draw water from public wells, seek admittance into schools and temples, and occupy public places.[64] Malaviya's close association with and influence on the Hindu Mahasabha ended in 1927 when, as we shall see, he developed some serious differences with its new president, B.S. Moonje.

Within Congress too, Malaviya stood up for Hindu interests whenever required. He was, as we have observed, unwilling to countenance the Lucknow Pact. He did not outright denounce it (we are not factoring in his oblique remarks at the aforementioned Banaras meeting of the

Hindu Mahasabha) only because it was supported by Bal Gangadhar Tilak (1856–1920).[65] Malaviya, it seems, had just too much respect for the Lokmanya and would not go against a scheme backed by him. However, when Congress failed to oppose the retention of separate electorates for Muslims under the 'Communal Award' in 1932, Malaviya openly rebelled. Eventually, after two years, he formed the Congress Nationalist Party (CNP) with Madhav Srihari Aney (1880–1968). Its objectives, as the two explained in a press note, were to organize a countrywide campaign against the Communal Award and 'field such candidates' in the elections who would reject it in the representative bodies.[66]

Malaviya, however, was not a 'communalist' in the sense of being hostile to Muslims or non-Hindus in general. He fell out with Moonje because he visualized a swaraj, or Indian self-rule, in which Hindus would be dominant.[67] This was thoroughly unacceptable to Malaviya. He considered Hindu–Muslim unity a precondition for the attainment of swaraj.[68] Naturally, this must mean that, in his view, Hindus and Muslims were to be equal citizens in swaraj. Furthermore, Malaviya urged his supporters to never disparage another religion. Instead, he demanded that they 'look with reverence at places of worship of other religions … speak with respect with followers of other religions, and give no cause of complaint in these respects'.[69] He subscribed to a 'high ideal of patriotism … [in which] Hindus, Mahomedans, Parsis and Christians, stand shoulder to shoulder as brothers and work for the common good of all'.[70] Malaviya's outlook, thus, was not tinged with sectarianism of any sort in the slightest. While remaining firm in his own Hindu religion, he was catholic and fair-minded towards every other. As he put it during his presidential address at the annual Congress session in Lahore in 1909:

> I am a Hindu by faith, and I mean no disrespect to any other religion when I say that I will not change my faith, for all the possessions of this world or of any other. (Cheers.) But I shall be a false Hindu, and I shall deserve less to be called a Brahman, if I desired that Hindus or Brahmans should have any unfair advantage as such over Mahomedans, Christians, or any other community in India. (Cheers.)[71]

Malaviya's Views on Education

Malaviya's family heritage had deeply immersed him in indigenous learning, while he also received the best of Western education. He was the liberal constitutionalist Congressman, as well as a champion of Hindu causes. Malaviya, in this way, combined an essentially secular approach towards politics with communitarian and cultural advocacy of various kinds. A deeply orthodox Hindu, he was completely bereft of enmity or prejudice against the adherents of other religions. He was an idealist, and he was a realist.[72]

An ardent patriot, Malaviya, as far as possible, be it as a lawyer or legislator, attempted to provide succour and redress to his compatriots through the legal and representative frameworks of the colonial administration. He, in other words, sought to pragmatically make the best of the means at his disposal to ensure that the alien regime is less of a scourge for Indians. Malaviya was deeply non-sectarian. He, as we have observed, had the seemingly innate capacity to consider two contrary positions and find a reasonable middle point between them. A profound sense of balance, thus, characterized Malaviya in every regard. We find this same sense in his views on education.

Having started his professional life as a schoolteacher, Malaviya was always something of an educationist. The instruction of Indians was a concern close to his heart, and he reflected upon it with a typical intellectual acuteness. Malaviya, in the process, as we shall see, came up with some well-formulated ideas on the issue.

Malaviya, as we have seen, favoured the 'vernacular', or the mother tongue, as the means of instruction. This was probably because he was taught in Hindi (along with Sanskrit), his first language, at the indigenous pathshalas he attended in childhood and found it an amenable experience. In the 'Court Character and Primary Education in the N.-W. Provinces & Oudh', thus, he strongly recommended that the colonial administration provide 'elementary education' in Hindi, 'the vernacular of the people', in the NWP&O, Bihar, and the Central Provinces.[73] Malaviya found Urdu 'utterly unsuited' as 'the medium of popular instruction' in these territories (just as he had found it so as the language of legal administration), since it preponderated 'with difficult foreign words and phrases' and was 'more or less alien to the people'.[74] On account of Urdu's strangeness and difficulty, Malaviya argued, a great deal of a pupil's time and energy were spent simply getting familiar with it, and they struggled to succeed academically. Those instructed in Hindi, on the other hand, in his view, did a lot better.[75]

While favouring elementary education in the vernacular, Malaviya also wanted it to be made free and compulsory. He, as a matter of fact, tabled a resolution in the Imperial

Legislative Council on 18 March 1910 demanding as much from the colonial administration:

> [A] beginning should be made in the direction of making elementary education free and compulsory throughout the country, and that a mixed Commission of officials and non-officials be appointed at an early date to frame definite proposals.[76]

Addressing the house subsequently, Malaviya attempted to allay the misgiving, apparently nurtured by some of his fellow legislators, that India was not yet ready for compulsory elementary education. His tone was both earnest and beseeching:

> I submit that every country that has emerged from the state of primitive barbarism is fit for a measure of elementary education. A country like this, where learning has from the highest times been highly appreciated, is most undoubtedly and pre-eminently fit for it.... The element of compulsion has been introduced and is at work in various forms and ways. Vaccination has been compulsory for a long time. And yet it is said that the country is not ripe for the gentle and humane measure of compulsory education, which will rescue the people from the darkness of ignorance, and from its evil concomitants, poverty, misery and crime![77]

Malaviya, to put it simply, thought that compulsory elementary education was fully apposite in the Indian context. The country, he appears to have concluded, would be receptive of the measure since a respect for learning was innate to its civilizational heritage. Furthermore, it seems to us, Malaviya wanted the colonial administration to be consistent and go the whole hog in making things compulsory for the public good. Thus, we find him declaiming that if vaccination could be compulsory so could be elementary education, all the more since its salutary effect on the country was likely to be wide ranging. To lend his demand greater cogency, Malaviya alluded to the 'striking progress' made by Japan and other countries, namely, Germany, France, Switzerland, and the USA after they made elementary education compulsory.[78]

The chronic erosion, and near disappearance, of the network of indigenous schools, it seems, was not lost on Malaviya. We, thus, see him ruefully bringing up the fact that 'out of every five villages, four are without a school' in India.[79] Malaviya, as we gather, thought that compulsory elementary education (needing the establishment of a large number of schools) would remedy this state of affairs. As he wound up his speech, he contended that the 'humble millions' of India would not have a 'life worthy to be called human' until they were secured 'the inestimable advantage of ... the blessed light of knowledge'[80] through compulsory elementary education. Denying human beings even a basic education, Malaviya appears to have thought, was to deny them their humanity.

Malaviya's family heritage and early schooling, as we understand, made him a strong advocate of indigenous knowledge. Thus, if the opportunity arose, he would try to get the colonial authorities to acknowledge its worth. For instance, on 9 March 1916, while speaking on a resolution seeking the training of medical students 'in the vernaculars' in the Imperial Legislative Council, Malaviya dwelt on the 'vast' and 'immeasurable' service rendered by the 'indigenous systems of medicine'. Untypically digressing from the nub of the resolution, he stressed 'the great need, insistent need, for the Government to recognize ... the justice of providing means for imparting instruction' in these systems.[81]

Some years later, as he addressed the Imperial Legislative Council 'regarding a grant of five lakhs ... to the Ayurvedic and Yunani Tibbi College, Delhi', Malaviya reiterated his confidence in the Indian systems of medicine and recommended that, if required, the government appoint a committee to verify their efficacy.[82] He was obviously very eager to allay any apprehensions or doubts the alien rulers might have had about the Indian science of healing.

There was, however, no dogmatic indigenism in Malaviya's educational philosophy. This is, once again, quite natural considering his academic background. After the pathshalas, as we saw, Malaviya attended an English-medium school and earned first a BA at Muir Central College and then an LLB at Allahabad University. To the greater extent, thus, he was shaped by Western education. Due to this reason, it seems, Malaviya was completely in favour of the Indian youths travelling to England, continental Europe, or the USA to get an education. He was not worried, as many were, that this might transform them culturally and cause them to end up maladjusted with their families. On the contrary, Malaviya thought that an education in the West would greatly benefit these youths by correctly moulding their characters and inculcating in them the capacity to battle life's troubles and difficulties.[83] Malaviya, thus, was completely unprejudiced against a foreign education.

He was also an ardent supporter of technical and industrial education which, he believed, was the basis of the prosperity of countries such as Germany, Japan, and the USA. As he understood, an 'extensive system of technical and industrial education' was similarly required in India to pull the 'vast millions' of its people out of poverty. Indians, according to Malaviya, lacked nothing in the way of intelligence, industriousness, and capacity for hard work. However, he observed that they did not have the requisite training and skills and were consequently 'beaten day by day by the manufacturers of every foreign country … [with] a system of technical education'. Foreign made goods, as a result, were flooding the Indian market. In 1909, thus, when he was elected Congress president for the first time, Malaviya appealed to the colonial administration to urgently adopt 'a system of technical education co-extensive with the needs of' India.[84]

Along with technical and industrial education, as his address on 'The Dacca University Bill' in the Imperial Legislative Council reveals, he was also keen on the promotion of commercial education and training in scientific agriculture in the country.[85] This, as we imagine, might have been because Malaviya thought these relatively new academic areas (as they were then) to be full of potential from the point of view of the national economy. When it came to education, he was truly a visionary thinker.

Malaviya, as we gather, considered a basic school-level education the right of every Indian and an imperative for social welfare and national advancement. One might say that he was something of a social democrat as an educationist (owing to his liberal political convictions). Besides, Malaviya desired an education system which represented and preserved the cultural heritage of the land. Hence, as we saw earlier, Malaviya wished for elementary education to be imparted in the vernacular and was extremely keen that the colonial administration arranged for instruction in the Indian systems of medicine.

At the same time, Malaviya was broad-minded enough to acknowledge the value of Western education (quite natural, considering he had received it himself), or the moral worth of an education abroad. He also saw education as a powerful means of national regeneration. Malaviya, thus, strongly championed the introduction of technical and industrial education in the country. He quite aptly grasped that that was the way to revive the Indian manufacturing capacity and alleviate the terrible poverty that plagued the land. Alongside, we find Malaviya acknowledging the value of an education in commerce and scientific agriculture. He, one might say, understood the full practical scope of education in terms of its utility in economic production and in training people for gainful employment with the appropriate skills.

Malaviya was, in this way, we shall argue, quite ahead of his times. His educational philosophy was remarkably holistic. It comprised a perfect balance of idealism and practical sense. Malaviya cannily combined two seemingly contradictory approaches towards education, just as he seamlessly blended two apparently contrary commitments in public life: towards liberal constitutionalism and Hindu activism.

The Scheme for a Hindu University

As we saw in the pervious chapter, the 'Wood's despatch' of 1854 resulted in universities to be established in the three Presidency capitals of Calcutta, Madras, and Bombay in 1857. They were meant to enable the 'diffusion of the improved arts, science, philosophy and literature of Europe;

in short of European knowledge' in India.[86] All colleges affiliated to them, thus, had to teach a broadly Western curriculum. Two more universities came up in British-ruled India over the remainder of the 19th century. The colonial administration established the Panjab University in 1882 and Allahabad University in 1887. Both, once again, enforced a generally Western curriculum on their affiliated colleges. Allahabad University, especially, emerged as a 'bastion of anglicization', neglecting the 'vernaculars ... and Indian academic subjects', and even 'refusing affiliation to any college that did not have a European principal'.[87] Thus, at the turn of the 20th century, there were a total of five universities in colonial India, and they all subserved the hegemony of the Western curriculum.

While the colonial university system was emergent in the second half of the 19th century, there were attempts on the part of Indians to establish institutions of higher education that represented and upheld the culture and heritage of the land (we are not considering the Hindu College established in 1817 since it imparted a predominantly Western curriculum). Overall, these attempts may be termed an aspect of the expansion of Indian initiative in the general paradigm of colonial education wherein, as we saw in the last chapter, both government and missionary agency were now on the wane. The Arya Samaj, for instance, founded several Dayanand Anglo-Vedic Colleges. First begun in Lahore, Ferozepur, and Multan, these institutions taught 'both the new knowledge of the anglicized world along with the Vedic truth'.[88] Again, the leaders of the Singh Sabha movement established the Khalsa College in Amritsar in 1892. It became, as Leah Renold puts it, 'the most important institution for the Sikhs, dedicated to the revival of Sikh religion through religious studies and literature'.[89] A few years afterwards, in 1898, Annie Besant began the Central Hindu College in the holy city of Banaras. Pupils at this institution were supposed to combine Western education with a study of the *shastras*.[90] Generally, however, these Indian initiatives did not make a tremendous difference to the existing higher education system. They were just too few, far between, and limited in scope. In this way, there was both a need and room for a significant Indian initiative within the colonial framework of higher education at the beginning of the 20th century.

Malaviya was no stranger to making an activist intervention in colonial academia as a Hindu. For instance, he was instrumental, by raising funds, behind the construction of the Hindu Boarding House at Allahabad University in 1901.[91] It provided Hindu students of the institution a dedicated residential space in conformity with their cultural mores and way of life. It seems that he hit upon the idea of a Hindu university at some point in 1903. Malaviya subsequently broached it to Maharaja Prabhu Narayan Singh (1855–1931) of Banaras, who had earlier been the president of the committee formed to oversee the construction of the Hindu Boarding House, leaving him 'over-whelmed with joy'.[92] With the ruler (even if symbolic) of the holy city on his side, Malaviya arranged a meeting to inaugurate his plan. Conducted at the Mint House, a hotel in Banaras, in early 1904, it was presided over by the Maharaja. Malaviya's idea of a Hindu university was 'received with great enthusiasm'[93] on the occasion. Its obvious attractiveness to the assembled Hindu notables apart, as we imagine, this could also have been due to the recent turn of events.

First, the Universities Commission appointed by the Viceroy, Lord Curzon (1859–1925), in 1902 was seeking to tighten official control over the existing universities (and reverse, to an extent, the retreat of governmental role in education). Second, the Mohammedan Anglo-Oriental Educational Conference, conducted the previous year in Bombay, had already raised the demand for a Muslim university.[94] The colonial administration exercising greater control over the universities was an apparent threat to whatever little elbow room the Indian-run affiliated colleges enjoyed. This obviously made the idea of a Hindu university, as far as possible free from governmental interference, very cogent. Mohammedan Anglo-Oriental Educational Conference's demand, on the other hand, had introduced and legitimized the idea of denominational universities in the colonial public sphere. Now the Hindus too could seek to have a university of their own.

Further, it is likely that the Mint House crowd was amenable to Malaviya because the university he had visualized was going to be a breakthrough in colonial higher education. None of the five universities of British-ruled India provided tuition. Their role was restricted to conducting examinations and supervising curriculum delivery in affiliated colleges. However, Malaviya had thought up a residential teaching university which would set its own curriculum. This must have come across as a remarkably novel and a very relevant idea.

Malaviya had already prepared the 'greater portion' of a prospectus to adumbrate the Hindu university when the meeting at the Mint House took place. After 'many months of discussion and deliberation', this text finally went to press in July 1905. Copies of it were sent to the 'leading Hindu gentlemen' of various provinces in October 1905. They, as we learn, 'warmly approved' of Malaviya's prospectus.[95]

Interestingly, the backdrop to this was the emerging Swadeshi movement in Bengal (against Lord Curzon's decision to partition the province into a Hindu-majority West Bengal and a Muslim-majority East Bengal). Along with the purchase and use of British-manufactured goods, its votaries were shunning the government-run educational institutions. For instance, a thousand students in Calcutta pledged to boycott them on 25 October 1905. Simultaneously, the leadership of the Swadeshi movement was endeavouring to create national educational institutions to replace the governmental ones. The likes of Bipin Chandra Pal (1858–1932), Maulvi Abdul Rasul (1872–1917), Shyam Sundar Chakrabarti (1869–1932), and Jnanendranath Roy, thus, planned to build a national university.[96]

In the light of these developments, Hindu notables in Bengal must have responded to Malaviya's prospectus with alacrity if they happened to read it. It is also likely that their counterparts in other provinces found it especially timely due to the tidings from Bengal.

The *Prospectus of a Proposed Hindu University for the Promotion of Scientific, Technical and Artistic Education Combined with Religious Instruction and Classical Culture* identified the 'relaxation' of the 'power of religion' among Hindus as the principal cause of their decline. Once a 'lofty and noble structure', the text lamented, Hindu society had been reduced to a 'shapeless heap'.[97] As it saw, the pursuit of religion among Hindus had come to be restricted to a 'few persons here and there'. Hindus possessing intellectual gifts were 'mostly absorbed in the cares of office or professional business', they hardly even thought of religion.

Similar was the case of wealthy and powerful Hindus. They, the prospectus complained, were 'engrossed in their temporal concerns ... [and had] little thought of the spiritual interests of their dependents or their neighbours, or even of their own'. The remainder of Hindu society comprised, as the text put it, 'ignorant agriculturists, petty traders, ill-trained artisans, half starved labourers, all forming a mass of abject humanity, oppressed by poverty and decimated by disease'. Malaviya, the author of the prospectus, obviously thought that these people were not equipped in any manner to bring about a Hindu renaissance. Overall, thus, in his view, Hindu society was in a very sorry state. He thought that Hindus were pursuing individual aims and that 'mutual trust and co-operation ... the very soul of ... corporate life' had all but disappeared from their midst.[98]

Malaviya prescribed a 'wide diffusion of knowledge' and the restoration of religion to its 'rightful place' in the fractured, ignorant, poor, and disease-stricken Hindu society. As he understood, ancient Hindus had prospered through a balanced pursuit of spiritual and practical goals.[99] He, thus, proposed the creation of a Hindu university that would combine religious instruction with the teaching of scientific, technical, and liberal arts subjects. It was, resultantly, visualized with the following five 'colleges' in the prospectus:

1. 'A College of Sanskrit Learning' that would teach the Vedas, Vedangas, Itihasas, and Puranas
2. 'An Ayurvedic College', featuring laboratories, a botanical garden, 'a firstclass hospital', and a veterinary department 'for improving the breeds of cattle and horses'
3. 'A College of Sthapatya Veda or Artha Shastra', with Departments of Physics and Chemistry and

a 'Technological Department for teaching the manufacture, by means of machinery, of the principal articles of personal and household use', as well as mining and metallurgy[100]

4. 'A College of Gandharva Veda and other fine arts', to impart knowledge of 'the dramatic art', 'painting and sculpture', and 'To preserve purity of design in the production of art wares, to arrest the spirit of slavish imitation of foreign models' and
5. 'A Linguistic College where students … [would] be taught English, and such other foreign languages as it may be found necessary to teach, in order to improve the Indian literature with all important sciences and arts.'[101]

The mediums of instruction at this residential university, with 'quarters for teachers and pupils',[102] were meant to be Sanskrit (for those who wished) and Hindi.[103] It would also prepare, Malaviya hoped, its own textbooks 'in Sanskrit and modern Indian languages' for its curriculum. However difficult, he argued in the prospectus, the task needed to be undertaken so that a 'vernacular literature' to serve as 'a medium of higher instruction' was generated.[104]

Malaviya recommended Banaras, 'from time immemorial … the centre of Hindu learning', as the seat of the eclectic Hindu university of his imagination. Also, he wanted it to overlook the river Ganga.[105] Malaviya 'proposed to invite all Hindu ruling chiefs, and nobles of high rank to become patrons of the institution, and to appoint their representatives in the governing body which … [would] be composed of the principal noblemen and gentlemen of the Hindu community in different parts of India'.[106] In other words, he sought to involve the Hindu elites from all over the country in the task of establishing this university. Malaviya's prospectus for a Hindu university, one might say, was a mirror reflection of his educational philosophy. It skilfully combined idealism and practical sense, an intention to preserve the civilizational heritage of the land while disseminating therein the best of contemporary Western learning and alleviate its misery and decay. This was indeed a prospectus authored by someone with a truly broad-ranging intellect capable of, as we concluded, combining the seemingly contrary.

The twenty-first annual session of the Congress took place in Banaras in 1905 from 27 to 30 December. Along with the Congress leadership and rank-and-file delegates, several eminent educationists arrived in the holy city to partake in the event. Malaviya used this opportunity to invite them to a meeting at the Town Hall of Banaras on 31 December. Representatives of Hindu society 'from almost every province of India' also participated in it. The foregoing prospectus of the Hindu university was discussed on the occasion and a committee was appointed to 'give final shape to it'.[107] Present on the occasion, Surendranath Banerjee (1848–1925) pledged the 'evening of his life' to the institution. Lokmanya Tilak, also in attendance, promised it 'three years of his life'.[108]

A few weeks later, Malaviya presented his scheme before the Sanatan Hindu Mahasabha (hereon only Mahasabha) when it assembled in Allahabad for the Kumbh Mela from 20 to 29 January under the presidency of Paramhans Parivrajakcharya Jagadguru Shankaracharya of Govardhan Math.[109] The religious body approved the proposal through a resolution that bestowed upon the proposed university its name and delineated its core mission:

I. That a Hindu university be established in Banaras under the name of the Bharatiya Vishvavidyalaya
   (a) To train teachers of religion for the preservation and promotion of Sanatan Dharma which is inculcated by the Srutis, Smritis and Puranas, and which recognizes *varna* and *asrama.*
   (b) To promote the study of the Sanskrit language and literature.
   (c) To advance and diffuse scientific and technical knowledge through the medium of Sanskrit and Indian vernaculars.[110]

A second resolution passed by the Mahasabha somewhat modified Malaviya's original plan regarding the Hindu university's academic structure and organization. It recommended that it have six colleges instead of five, namely, 'A Vaidic College', 'An Ayurvedic (Medical) College', 'A Department of Chemistry', 'A Technological Department', 'An Agricultural College', and 'A College of Gandharva Veda'. The Mahasabha adopted a further resolution illustrating its vision for the Hindu university's interiority, or essential nature. As these Sadhus and Shastris,[111] and their leader, the Shankaracharya, thought, it ought to represent, to a reasonable extent, the traditional Hindu social mores while also being an inclusive space:

II. (a) That the Vedic college and all the religious work of the university be under the control of Hindus who accept and follow the principles of the Sanatan Dharma as laid down in the Srutis, Smritis and Puranas;
   (b) That admission to this College be regulated in accordance with the rules of the Varnasrama Dharma;

(c) That all other Colleges be open to students of all creeds and classes; and the secular branches of Sanskrit learning be also taught without restriction of caste and creed.[112]

The Mahasabha, thus, broadly agreed with Malaviya's conception of the Hindu university as an institution simultaneously preserving civilizational heritage and propagating Western learning. It only added a bit to this conception from its own conservative point of view (asking for the observance of scriptures and Varnashrama Dharma at the Vedic college) while favourably vetting it. The Mahasabha did not seriously disturb the progressive, forward-looking outlook at the central core of Malaviya's vision for the Hindu university. The organization, as we observe, was quite amenable to it.

Malaviya's idea of the Hindu university received positive responses all along. Apparently, a broad consensus in its support had emerged amongst the contemporary Hindu leadership, both in politics and in religious and spiritual affairs. Nothing, however, came out of it immediately. When Malaviya submitted his prospectus before the United Provinces government for consideration, it received a most unfavourable response. This was chiefly because the Governor of the province, Sir John Hewett (1854–1941), thought that there was 'no room for a teaching university in India'. He also found the idea of a 'Hindu denominational university' highly 'undesirable'.[113] Malaviya could not proceed to give concrete shape to his plan without the cooperation of the provincial administration. The Swadeshi movement too claimed his attentions and he had to keep postponing an 'organized endeavour' to establish the Hindu university for the subsequent few years.[114]

3

BHU: The Inception (1911–15)

The 'University of India'

Annie Besant, an Englishwoman from London, was a passionate votary of Indian culture and spirituality. This was, as we understand, due to her involvement with the Theosophical Society. Besant met Madame Blavatsky (1831–91), one of its founders, in 1882. Impressed, it seems, by her spirituality and mysticism, Besant eventually joined the society in 1889. As an intellectual and spiritual outlook, Theosophy sought to challenge the 'sense of rationalist superiority of the West' by rediscovering and rehabilitating 'all that was great and glorious'[1] in Eastern thought. Understandably, thus, a committed Theosophist like Besant was drawn towards India, a country with an abundantly rich spiritual and philosophical heritage. She arrived in the country in 1893 and made it her home.

The current degraded state of India, with its population mired in squalor, poverty, and illiteracy, pained her immensely. Besant dearly wanted this ancient land to reclaim its former resplendence and glory.[2] She, resultantly, undertook to help it through tireless political and cultural activism. Besant, as we saw in the previous chapter, championed Indian Home Rule. Although of the rulers' race, she was extremely vocal about Indians' right to rule themselves.

Besant was also an educationist. She, as we surmise, believed that the right education, replete with religious and moral training, was the key to alleviate the miserable condition India had fallen into. Hence, she established the Central Hindu College in 1898. Affiliated to the Allahabad University, it began functioning with 'fifteen teachers and 177 students'.[3] The institution did some pioneering work towards collating and setting down the essentials of the Hindu religion in an accessible form. As we learn, the Central Hindu College issued the Sanatan Dharma Series of 'Hindu religious text-books' in 1902. These comprised a 'Catechism', an 'Elementary Text-Book', and an 'Advanced Text-Book'.[4] Apparently well compiled and written, these books 'received the approbation of eminent Pundits throughout India'.[5] The Central Hindu College, thus, seriously set about to preserve the Indian spiritual and philosophical heritage and bring it to the educated Indians. Besant's brainchild, in this way, worked to reenergize pride in India's civilizational past and reinvigorate Indian society.

Although a Hindu, Besant, it appears to us, was quite catholic in temperament and open-minded towards other spiritual traditions. We must be mindful that, regardless of her background, she was an Indian nationalist. Resultantly, it was all the more natural for her to exhibit this catholicity of temperament. Along with the Hinduism she had embraced, Besant was accepting of every religion that her adopted country was home to. She, thus, we discover, was thinking in terms of an all-denominational 'University of India' by 1907. As conceived by Besant, its 'Trustees and representatives' were to be from 'all the important creeds' prevalent in India. Starting off as an examining university, the University of India, she had thought, would eventually provide tuition and 'affiliate Colleges of all denominations'.[6] This was to be, thus, a trailblazing institution with a truly national scope.

Annie Besant

Source: Wikimedia Commons

With the objective of securing a Royal Charter of Incorporation for the University of India, Besant drafted a rather detailed petition addressing the colonial administration. It was, we are told, referred to the Secretary of State for India by the Viceroy in 1910. The former, in turn, sent the petition for the consideration of the Government of India.[7] Early in this text, as we see, Besant had limned her vision for the all-denominational university in terms of its organizational structure and intent. She informed the colonial regime,

> The most marked speciality of the proposed University … [would] lie in the fact that it …[would] affiliate no College in which religion and morality do not form an integral part of the education given; it … [would] make no distinction between religionsaccepting equally Hindū, Būḍḍhist, Pārsī, Christian and Muhammaḍan, but it … [would] not affiliate no purely secular institution. It … [would] supply a gap in the educational system of India, and … draw together all the elements which regard the training of youth in honor and virtue, the most essential part of education.[8]

Besant, thus, desired to provide a counter and remedy for the total absence of religious and moral training in contemporary Indian education through the University of India. She also, it seems, was envisioning the institution as a rallying ground for individuals from all over the country who wished the same as her and build it up as a nationalist endeavour. Besides imparting knowledge of religion and morality, the University of India was also to introduce students to the liberal arts within a distinctly Indic framework. As Besant wrote in the petition, this would be the 'second important speciality' of the institution. It would place 'in the first rank '... Indian philosophy, history, and literature, and ... [seek] in these, and in the classical languages of India, the chief means of culture'. Besant reassured the colonial authorities that the University of India would not ignore Western thought and study it 'amply'. However, it would give the 'lead' to its Eastern counterpart and use 'western knowledge ... to enrich, but not to distort or cripple the expanding national life'.[9]

Thus, the institution Besant had conceived of was to selectively focus on only as much Western learning as she thought was genuinely required, no more. Being sensible in this way, the University of India did not mean to ignore the scientific and technical knowledge of the West due to its obvious utility from the point of view of economic production. Imparting this knowledge was going to be the 'third important speciality' of the institution. Thus, Besant's petition declared that the University of India would pay 'special attention to manual and technical training, to science applied to agriculture and manufacture ... [and] bring from the West all that can be usefully assimilated for the increasing of national prosperity'.[10]

Overall, thus, as we deduce, Besant had imagined the University of India as an institution rooted in Indian heritage and working for national regeneration. Larger in both scale and scope, addressing all Indian society and not just one religious group therein, it would have been a natural step up for Besant from the Central Hindu College. The ambitious University of India, unfortunately, failed to materialize.

While the colonial authorities were mulling over Besant's petition, activism for a Muslim university had picked up pace and met with considerable success. Instead of starting from scratch, Muslim leaders were now energetically attempting to build up the Mohammedan Anglo-Oriental College at Aligarh (established in 1875 by Syed Ahmad Khan [1817–98]) as a university.[11] Furthermore, they had managed to raise Rs 25 lakh that the regime had made a precondition for considering a Charter of Incorporation for a Muslim university.[12]

Finding, it appears, their own denominational university in sight, the Muslim signatories to Besant's petition withdrew their support for an all-denominational university. The proposed University of India, in this way, ceased to represent all of India's religious groups and lost its raison d'etre. At this point, Besant decided to join hands with Malaviya, since the two of them were thinking on similar lines. Both, after all, wanted to establish a university which would combine secular education with instruction in religion and morality and preserve the Indian epistemic heritage.

Thus, Besant and Malaviya met in Calcutta in March 1911 and amalgamated their schemes. They had a second meeting on 8 April and decided that the petition Besant had originally submitted regarding the University of India shall be the basis of their undertaking, albeit in a modified form. Subsequently, Besant issued a circular on 11 April and formally announced the amalgamation of her scheme with Malaviya's. She also revealed to have modified her original proposal so that it was now about securing the 'University of Benares' or 'Kashi Vishvavidyalaya'. This institution was to be built around the already existing Central Hindu College in the holy city.[13]

Besant and Malaviya, however, could not immediately put together a detailed proposal regarding the university they had decided to partner for. On 22 April, Besant boarded a steamer for England. As it turned out, she remained there for six months.[14]

Malaviya Resumes Efforts for a Hindu University

While Besant came over to his side, Malaviya resumed his activism for the project he had had to abandon a few years ago with renewed urgency. He had expressed the wish to do so once in 1908,[15] and again in 1910 at the twenty-fifth annual session of the Congress.[16] On both occasions, however, he had failed to follow up. The reason Malaviya was finally stirred into action, we imagine, was the headway the Muslim side had managed to make with its own university scheme.

Madan Mohan Malaviya

Source: Wikimedia Commons

We, consequently, find him writing a letter to the Maharaja of Darbhanga on 6 April 1911 and pressing upon him the necessity of raising 'sufficient funds ... at the earliest possible date' to obtain a Charter of Incorporation for a Hindu university 'on the same conditions as the Muhammadans'. As he wound up the epistle, Malaviya requested the Maharaja to 'take the lead' in the matter.[17]

Malaviya reiterated the request in another letter to Rameshwar Singh on 15 April. He also informed the potentate about having met with Besant.[18] Apparently, this was an allusion to the meeting in which the two had combined their projects. Malaviya, it appears to us, was keen to secure the involvement of the Maharaja of Darbhanga at the forefront of the efforts for a Hindu university since he himself desired to establish a Sanskrit university in Banaras. Rameshwar Singh intended to call this institution 'Sarada Vishwavidyalaya'.[19]

Malaviya, it is very likely, trusted the Maharaja to understand his vision and saw in him the ideal royal ally (who would come in handy when dealing with the colonial authorities and eliciting largesse and support from the princely states). He was not disappointed. Like Besant, Rameshwar Singh merged his scheme with Malaviya's and, as we shall see, dedicatedly championed the cause of the Hindu university.

An unexpected obstacle came in the way of Malaviya in the form of orthodox unease towards Besant. They were worried lest she impose Theosophy on the University of Benares when it is established and divert it from Sanatan Dharma.[20] The orthodox were also unconformable with the veritable cult she was building around J. Krishnamurthy (1895–1986), then a boy prodigy, terming him the

Maharaja Rameshwar Singh

Source: Wikipedia

'world teacher'. Further, it is likely that they were concerned about the actual extent to which the university Besant and Malaviya were striving for would be Hindu, since the former had originally set out to establish an all-denominational university.

Bharat Dharm Mahamandal, interestingly patronized by none other than the Maharaja of Darbhanga, took the lead in censuring Besant.[21] The orthodox fears, it appears, found enough traction to be echoed in the vernacular press. The Hindi monthly *Maryada*, for instance, alluded to the strong objection nurtured by a 'certain party' against the merger of the University of India and Hindu university schemes.[22]

A pious and observant Hindu himself, Malaviya, of course, could not remain indifferent to the misgivings of the orthodox. Again, he might have been concerned about retaining the confidence of Rameshwar Singh. The Bharat Dharm Mahamandal's disapproval of Besant, it is quite possible, was due to the Maharaja's displeasure with her.

Malaviya, therefore, met with the members of the Central Hindu College Committee on 10 July 1911 and 'pointed out certain difficulties that presented themselves to his mind and the minds of some of his friends in connection with the amalgamated scheme'.[23] He, we imagine, was worried that it conveyed no clear commitment to the creation of a university explicitly Hindu in character.

The next day, Malaviya wrote a letter to Besant and told her about the 'uncompromising' opposition of the 'men of orthodox views' against the amalgamated scheme. Some 'advanced social reformers', too, he added, were opposed to it. Apparently, regardless of social and religious attitudes, a considerable mass of Hindu notables had allied against the measure. Nevertheless, Malaviya told Besant that there is a second party which 'sincerely desires' a merger of their respective schemes.[24] The majority of it, he wrote, expected the university that is established to be 'a distinctly Hindu University'.

Malaviya, as a result, emphasized that its name must bear out the fact that it is a Hindu institution. Calling it the 'University of Benares' in place of the 'University of India', thus, he declared, would not suffice, since neither name guaranteed that the institution would not be all-denominational in character. Malaviya explained to Besant that they would not be justified in appealing to Hindus to regard an all-denominational institution as 'peculiarly belonging to their community'.[25] Neither, he wrote, would they be able to make any special claims upon their 'sympathy and support' for its sake.[26]

A few days later, on 15 July, Malaviya announced his concerns in the *Leader* newspaper.[27] Perhaps, this was his bid to demonstrate to those ranged against the amalgamated scheme that he was sincerely working to establish a Hindu university.

On 6 August, Malaviya participated in the half-yearly meeting of the Board of Trustees of the Central Hindu College and stressed the need to modify the amalgamated plan in view of the 'new circumstances'.[28] He, it seems, was trying to ensure that it contains an unambiguous commitment to establishing a Hindu university. The Board of Trustees, however, only stopped at a resolution promising 'full cooperation' to Malaviya and Besant in securing a 'Hindu University at Benares of which the Central Hindu College shall form an integral portion'.[29]

It is likely that these gentlemen subsequently informed Besant, then in England, about their conversation with Malaviya. Apparently piqued by his continuing trepidations regarding the University of Benares scheme, she wrote a rather testily worded letter to the *Advocate*, a periodical published from Lucknow, making clear her intention to go ahead with it:

> I am … proceeding with the scheme … agreed to. I cannot agree to throwing aside the scheme worked for, for several

> years, approved by the Viceroy and forwarded by him to the Secretary of State for India ... I have discussed with the Marquess of Crewe [Robert Crewe-Milnes (1858–1945), Secretary of State] the modification in the original scheme, and the change of name from the 'University of India' to the 'University of Benares' necessitated by the demand for a Muslim University ... On my return to India, I shall work to raise funds. I make this statement in order that all my friends in India may know that I do not agree to drop my nearly completed work, as the Hon. Pandit seems to expect.[30]

Besant, it seems, was not aware that Malaviya had already drafted and circulated a prospectus for a categorically Hindu university. It was, by and large, a revised version of the prospectus he had released in 1905. Malaviya had stolen a march on Besant.

The Revised Prospectus

Malaviya, as we discover, had completed authoring this document by July 1911.[31] Titled *The Hindu University of Benares: Why It Is Wanted and What It Aims At*, it provided a detailed outline of the institution he had in mind in terms of its relevance and objectives. Malaviya, to begin with, termed it a 'residential and teaching University of the modern type'. He pointed out that no university of this kind currently existed in India, as the five existing universities in the country were 'mainly examining Universities'. Malaviya conceded that they had 'done and ... [were] doing most useful work'. However, he felt that there was the need

> for a University which ... [would] teach as well as examine, and which by reason of ... being a residential University, ... [would] realize the ideal of University life as it was known

> in the past in India, and as … known in the advanced countries of the West.

Malaviya, thus, was fleshing out an institution in the image of the Taxila and Nalanda universities of yore as well as the contemporary Western universities. His was, in this way, an eclectic vision. The eclecticism of Malaviya's vision became further apparent as he proceeded to enumerate the objectives of the Hindu University of Benares:

> (i) To promote the study of the Hindu Shastras and of Samskrit [sic] literature generally … and all that was good and great in the ancient civilization of India;
> (ii) to promote learning and research generally in arts and science in all branches;
> (iii) to advance and diffuse such scientific, technical and professional knowledge, combined with the necessary practical training, as it is best calculated to help in promoting indigenous industries and in developing the material resources of the country; and
> (iv) to promote the building up of character in youth by making religion and ethics an integral part of education.[32]

The new prospectus, thus, echoed the previous one in describing a university that would impart a judicious blend of Indian and practically useful Western learning and include the religious and moral dimensions of Hinduism in the curriculum. In this way, the second prospectus articulated Malaviya's idealism and practical sense the same way as the first. However, when it came to picturing the academic organization of this institution, it diverged from its predecessor. In the revised prospectus, Malaviya visualized the Hindu University of Benares with the following 'Colleges':

1) A Samskrit College with a theological department;
2) A College of Arts and Literature;
3) A College of Science and Technology;
4) A College of Agriculture;
5) A College of Commerce;
6) A College of Medicine; and
7) A College of Music and the Fine Arts.[33]

Malaviya, as we find, had scaled up his ambition regarding the institution he wanted to establish, since the first prospectus had proposed no more than five colleges. To an extent, one infers, this was due to the recommendations of the Sanatan Hindu Mahasabha. Two new colleges that Malaviya was envisioning this time, namely, that of 'Science and Technology' and agriculture are clearly traceable to its Allahabad resolution. With these Malaviya had teamed the colleges of 'Arts and Literature' and commerce, entirely new conceptions both. As such, only the colleges of 'Sanskrit Learning' and 'Gandharva Veda and other fine arts' had made it into the second prospectus from the first, albeit with rather altered names. The 'College of Medicine', as we shall see, may not be termed a retention from the first prospectus or derived from the Mahasabha's resolution, since it intended to teach a blend of Western and Indian medicine. It was not anymore about Ayurveda alone. Generally, compared to the last time, Malaviya was envisaging an institution with a more wide-ranging academic scope.

The Samskrit College, the prospectus declared, would make 'satisfactory provision' for the teaching of the Vedas.[34] On the other hand, 'languages, comparative philology, philosophy, history, political economy, pedagogy, & c.', were going to be taught at the College of Arts and Literature. Primarily, thus, its focus was to be on the liberal arts. Malaviya proposed to make the Central Hindu College 'the nucleus' of this college.

As about the College of Science and Technology, he wanted it to comprise 'four well-equipped departments of pure and applied sciences'. This was because, Malaviya wrote, 'no branch of education' was more needed than 'scientific and technical instruction' in view of the economic condition of India.[35] As he understood, 'for the salvation of the country from many … economic evils', it was an imperative to divert a 'substantial portion of the population from agricultural to industrial pursuits'. This, Malaviya observed, necessitated 'the multiplication of the existing facilities of technical and industrial education'.[36] The Hindu University of Benares, thus, he hoped, would alleviate the wretched poverty of the Indian masses, mostly deriving a meagre livelihood from agriculture, by disseminating in their midst the knowledge of industrial production.

Malaviya, however, expected agriculture to remain the dominant economic activity in India regardless of the development of 'manufacturing industries'. This made the College of Agriculture in his eyes particularly relevant. As he put it, 'The greatest service that can be rendered to the teeming millions of this country is to make two blades of grass grow where only one grows at present.'[37] Apparently, the College of Agriculture was going to do precisely this through 'the study of agricultural science'.[38]

The fifth college at the Hindu University of Benares, the College of Commerce, the prospectus announced, would provide 'special training for the young men … [intending] to devote themselves to commercial practices....' It was, in other words, going to be a 'business school'. Malaviya saw that 'commercial education' was 'fully recognized' as a 'factor in the national and international progress ... in the advanced countries of the West'.[39] He, therefore, as we gather, wanted the Hindu University of Benares to impart this education and contribute to national advancement.

The College of Medicine was an answer to the chronic lack of medical practitioners in the country.[40] It was, however, Malaviya promised, not going to focus on Western medicine alone. Its 'distinguishing feature', he wrote, would be imparting 'Hindu medical science ... along with the European system of medicine and surgery'.[41] The College of Medicine would also, Malaviya promised, enrich the former with the 'marvelous achievements which modern medical science has made in anatomy, physiology, surgery and all the other departments of the healing art, both on the preventive and the creative side'. In this way, it aimed 'to provide the country with *Vaidyas* well-qualified as both physicians and surgeons'.

Finally, the College of Music and the Fine Arts, the prospectus said, would 'recover the world of beauty and sublimity which was reared in *ragas*', 'encourage painting and sculpture', and 'preserve and promote purity of design in the promotion of art wares, to arrest the spirit of slavish imitation of foreign models'.[42] Mostly, as we see it, the colleges at the Hindu University of Benares were meant to build up the country by addressing its needs and deficiencies.

Besides seeking to create a university with more colleges or academic departments, the new prospectus differed from the first in another vital point, namely, the medium of instruction. Previously, Malaviya had wanted it to be primarily Hindi. This time, however, he had given up this desire due to the 'absence of suitable treatises and text books on science' in the language. He had also come to think that making Hindi the medium of instruction in the Hindu University of Benares would hinder it from drawing students from all over the country. Therefore, the revised prospectus concluded that teaching at the institution ought to be done in the English language.

Nonetheless, it looked forward to a time when the 'vernaculars are gradually developed' and the university may 'allow any one or more of them to be used as the medium of instruction'. Even then, Malaviya assured, due to 'the great usefulness of the English language as a language of worldwide utility … [it] shall … be taught as a second language'.[43] The Hindu University of Benares, thus, would not make the medium of instruction such that it impedes its students from accessing scientific learning, or restricts its intake of students only to a certain part of India. Malaviya, as we understand, wanted to establish an institution free from the tinge of intellectual provincialism and truly representative of the entirety of Hindu society.

After dwelling on the matter of the medium of instruction, Malaviya elaborated as to why, in his view, a residential teaching university was needed in the country. The 'Indian experience of the last fifty years,' he thought, '[had] proved that a system which … [provided] merely for examining students … and…[did] not at the same time compel them to study … systematically under first-rate instruction, … [tended] inevitably to accentuate certain characteristic defects of the Indian intellect'. These were, Malaviya observed, 'the development of memory out of all proportion to the other faculties of the mind, the incapacity to observe and appreciate facts, and the taste for metaphysical and technical distinctions'.[44] The Hindu University of Benares was required to remedy this state of affairs. It would not, the prospectus implied, enforce rote learning on students but train them to independently apprehend phenomena. It would also emancipate their minds from the proclivity for needless hair-splitting and pedantry. Another compelling reason necessitated this institution. Malaviya felt that 'a mere examining University … [did] little to promote the formation of character, which … is even more important for the well-being of the individual and of the community, than the cultivation of intellect'. 'These and similar considerations,' thus, he concluded, pointed 'to the necessity of establishing residential and teaching Universities in India of the type … [existing] in all the advanced countries of the West'. Fitting the description, the Hindu University of Benares, resultantly, would 'supply a distinct want … recognized both by the Government and the public, and … prove a most valuable addition to the educational institutions of the country'.[45]

It would be a place forging the character of young Hindus so that they turn out to be 'men of … probity and honor, whose conduct through life … [shows] that they bear the hallmark of a great University'.[46] The Hindu University of Benares aimed to do so by introducing them to the 'noble teachings' of their religion. This was evident, given that these teachings included:

> truthfulness, integrity, fortitude; self-help, self-respect, self-control, abstinence from injury, forgiveness, compassion; philanthropy, hospitality, unselfish action for public good,

> reverence for age and authority, discipline and devotion to duty, and above all, the service of God through the service of man and friendliness to the whole creation.

Malaviya pointed out that Hinduism is replete with 'all the virtues which elevate human character, support human society, and promote peace on earth and good-will among men'. 'Hindu philosophy' and 'Hindu religious literature', he further averred, lead 'man into the path of righteousness' and teach him 'that every creature around him is his own self in another guise, and that he rises in the scale of being by doing good to those with whom he comes in contact and degrades himself by injuring his fellow creatures'.[47] Students arriving at the Hindu University of Benares, in this way, stood to become better human beings through immersion in a set of profoundly beautiful spiritual and moral values.

The First Fundraising Drive: Formation of the 'Hindu University Society'

Malaviya made an appeal for funds to establish the Hindu University of Benares on 15 July 1911. He estimated that the actualization of this institution required Rs 1 crore. Malaviya wanted to raise Rs 50 lakh, or half of this amount, before King George V (1865–1936) visited India in December to preside over the 'Delhi Durbar'.[48] Again, he targeted to collect Rs 20 lakh of this sum by September and, if possible, request a Charter of Incorporation for the university from the government.[49]

Apparently, the idea playing in his mind was to coincide the foundation stone laying ceremony of the Hindu University of Benares with the Delhi Durbar.[50] He might have thought that this would earn the institution a vivid place in the public imagination and ease the flow of funds and patronage towards it.

The sharp deadlines Malaviya set himself in the way of fundraising indicate the great importance he attached to the cause he was championing. Due to this reason, it seems, Malaviya worded his appeal in a way that it resonated with Hindus of both considerable and relatively modest means. Targeting a broad social pool of potential donors, Malaviya asked for sums of 'any size from one lac [sic] down to ten rupees'.[51] Accompanied by Hindu notables, he began a fundraising tour of multiple towns and cities towards the end of July. Addressing public meetings at these places, he tried to galvanize Hindus into making generous contributions for their own denominational university at Banaras.

The first town Malaviya visited was Faizabad, on 28 July.[52] The next month was especially busy for him. On 17 and 18 August, he was at Bankipur. He went to Gorakhpur on 21 August.[53] 26–27 August Malaviya spent in Kanpur. He then stayed at Muzaffarpur from 29–30 August and travelled to Darbhanga on the last day of the month.[54] Subsequently, after visiting Lucknow on 3 September,[55] Malaviya arrived in Calcutta on 5 September. The next day, 'a very influential and representative meeting of the citizens' of the then capital of British India 'was held at the Town-Hall to consider the Hindu University scheme'. With Dr Rash Behari Ghosh (1845–1921) presiding, seemingly spontaneous resolutions were adopted in its favour. More importantly, 'Five lakhs of rupees were subscribed on the spot'.[56]

Rising to speak amid 'deafening cheers', Malaviya deplored the physical and mental degeneration of the 'Hindu nation'. He observed that Hindus needed education 'to improve their condition'. To this end, Malaviya held up the vision of a

'Hindu University' combining a 'secular and religious' curriculum before his audience. He assured them that it would not 'impart sectarian education'. The import of his remark might have been that instruction at the university would not be as per the tenets of a particular sect of Hindus alone. Malaviya promised an institution welcoming 'all Hindus from the Himalayas to Cape Comorin' and concluded by making a 'most moving appeal for funds'[57] for its sake. He next went to Faridpur in eastern Bengal on 9 September.[58] A fortnight later, on the twenty-fourth of the month, he returned to Calcutta for a second round of fundraising.[59]

Malaviya visited Amritsar on 30 September at the invitation of the Punjab Hindu Conference. He and the deputation accompanying him were accorded a 'most cordial welcome' at the railway station with shouts of '*Hindu Dharm ki jai*' ('victory to Hindu religion') and '*Hindu University ki jai*' ('victory to Hindu University').[60] There was certainly considerable excitement in the town regarding the university Malaviya had come to seek funds for. Later, addressing a public meeting in a pandal (a temporary canvass pavilion) 'for about an hour', he emphasized that the 'secular education … being imparted in Government schools and colleges required to be supplemented by religious education'. Malaviya also stressed 'the necessity of preserving the best Hindu ideals, the best of the Hindu traditions, in short the best of Hindu culture and civilization'. To ensure that these objectives are met, 'He appealed to the [assembled] public to contribute their mite so that in the sacred city of Benares, five miles away from the inhabited part, a Hindu University might come into existence.'[61]

Malaviya reached Lahore on 8 October[62] after a stop at Rawalpindi (on 5 October).[63] Once again, he and his companions were received with tremendous enthusiasm. Malaviya was invited to address a public meeting at Bradlaugh Hall the next day. All 'available space' at the venue was occupied much before 7 a.m., when the event was scheduled to begin. Even 'doors, windows and approaches to the platform were thickly packed with men'. As soon as Malaviya and his companions appeared on stage, 'the hall resounded with loud and prolonged cheers'.[64] These denizens of Lahore, we imagine, must have been very keenly looking forward to the establishment of a Hindu university at Benares. Present on the occasion, Gopal Krishna Gokhale (1866–1915) 'expressed his full sympathy with the movement for ... [the institution] and promised to contribute Rs 5,000/- towards its funds'.[65]

The 'Hindu citizens' of Amritsar persuaded Malaviya to address a second public meeting in their town on the same day as the Bradlaugh Hall meeting. We do not know at what hour it was conducted. Considering that Malaviya had to travel from Lahore to arrive at this event, it must have been sometime in the afternoon or evening. 'Over 3000 Hindus' attended it. Not just participation, but from the fundraising point of view too this public meeting was a noteworthy success with subscriptions 'amounting to Rs 70,000/-' being announced.[66]

Rameshwar Singh, Malaviya's royal associate, meanwhile, was doing his own bit for the Hindu University of Benares. On 10 October, we find him writing a probing letter to Sir Harcourt Butler, Member for Education on the Viceroy's Executive Council. Rameshwar Singh, as we observe, was trying to find out about the conditions on which the colonial authorities might be willing to grant a Hindu denominational university. He began by pointing out to Butler the 'widespread feeling amongst the Hindu public to establish a Hindu University'.[67] Due to this reason, he wrote, he thought it was 'necessary' to get from him a 'clear indication of the lines on which Government … [would] be prepared to support the idea of a Hindu University'. The Maharaja of Darbhanga concluded the letter with the assurance that Hindus would 'be only too happy to loyally carry out any directions that Government may be pleased to give them and … [would] thankfully accept any suggestions' that Butler 'may be pleased to make'.[68]

Sir Harcourt Butler

Source: Wikimedia Commons

We may ascribe the rather ingratiating tone of this epistle to Rameshwar Singh's deep commitment to the cause of the Hindu university—he earnestly wanted it to see the light of the day—and the fact that, as a 'native ruler,' he required to be in the good graces of the colonial authorities to occupy the throne.

Butler wrote his reply on 12 October. In the 'absence of definite and detailed schemes' (apparently, the revised prospectus Malaviya had prepared did not count), he said, he could do no more than 'indicate certain conditions' on which the 'Government of India' might be willing to grant a 'Hindu University'. These were:

(1) The Hindus should approach Government in a body as the Mahommadans did;
(2) A strong efficient and financially sound college with an adequate European staff should be the basis of the Scheme;
(3) The University should be a modern University, mainly in being a teaching and residential University and offering religious instruction;
(4) The movement should be entirely educational;
(5) There should be the same measure of Government supervision and opportunity to give advice as in the case of the proposed University at Aligarh.

Butler, it seems, was telling Rameshwar Singh that the demand for a denominational university, to sound persuasive to the government, must appear to articulate a social consensus among Hindus. Which is why his first instruction that they approach the regime 'in a body'. The subsequent advice that he gave to the Maharaja of Darbhanga, we surmise, indicate his concern lest the proposed institution turn out to be too nationalist or indigenist. He did not want a Hindu university that would give the government cause for concern in the way of being excessively assertive about its cultural identity and unwilling to submit to any form of control. Butler concluded by emphasizing that adequate funds must be collected to 'satisfy' the 'Government of India and the Secretary of State … [regarding] the suitability in all particulars of the constitution of the University'. Finally, and very importantly, he promised Rameshwar Singh his and his department's 'ungrudging co-operation' in the pursuit of this goal.[69]

Rameshwar Singh, Malaviya, and a deputation of notables revealed the contents of Butler's letter at a public meeting in Meerut on 17 October. The event elicited a very enthusiastic response. 'The demand for seats was such that about 10,000 people were occupying the' *pandal* 'long before the appointed time'. As Rameshwar Singh read out the correspondence between him and the highest authority in charge of education in British-ruled India, there were 'deafening cheers'. A certain Rana Sheoraj Singh subsequently moved the following resolution:

> That this meeting begs to express its deep satisfaction at the assurance which the Government of India has been pleased to give that they will support the Hindu University movement under the conditions laid down by the Hon. Mr Butler … and tenders its thanks to his Excellency the Viceroy and the Hon. Mr Butler for the kindly interest they have taken in the movement.[70]

Malaviya rose to deliver an address after the regime had been appropriately thanked for being positively disposed towards the demand for a Hindu denominational university. He 'referred at length to the various stages through which the Hindu University movement had passed' and (expectedly) concluded by making 'an eloquent appeal for funds' to ensure its success. As though on cue, the Maharaja of Darbhanga stood up and 'announced his magnificent donation of five lakhs for the Hindu University'. Several local notables followed with their own donations, none quite inconsiderable.[71] Especially noteworthy was the contribution of Meerut's Sangeet Samaj. This ensemble of theatre artists donated the Rs 10,000 it had raised by performing a play on the virtuous king Harishchandra.[72] The public meeting at Meerut, thus, was a significant success from the fundraising point of view.

Besant was back in India on 21 October. She, Malaviya, and Rameshwar Singh met in Banaras the next day. The mild acrimony that we saw creeping in between Besant and Malaviya had by now dissipated. The former was not, after all, unilaterally proceeding with her University of Benares scheme. She had also come around to Malaviya's vision of a determinately Hindu institution of higher education. With their differences settled and visions aligned, the two of them drew up a memorandum of truly momentous significance on 22 October. It read as follows:

1) That the name of the University shall be Hindu University.
2) That the first governing body shall consist of the representatives of the Hindu community, Mrs Annie Besant and representative trustees of the C.H.C. [Central Hindu College].
3) The Theological faculty shall be entirely in the hands of Hindus.

4) That the C.H. College shall be incorporated with the University.
5) That the petition for a Charter now before the Secretary of State for India shall be withdrawn.

Besant, in other words, formally consented to merge the Central Hindu College into the would-be Hindu denominational university. Furthermore, she agreed that the administrative control of this institution would chiefly rest with Hindus, while Hindus alone would provide religious instruction there. Besant also proceeded to retract the original petition she had submitted to the colonial authorities, first seeking a Charter for the University of India and later for the University of Benares. She, thus, we might say, came to unambiguously endorse the idea of a Hindu university at Banaras.

About a month later, on 20 November, Besant and Malaviya formed the Hindu University Society (HUS) in Allahabad, mainly to transact the financial affairs concerning the establishment of a Hindu University within a formal organizational framework.[73] The body was registered on 15 December. Its office was opened at 4, Couper Road, Allahabad, on the first day of 1912. Rai Bahadur Sir Sundar Lal (1857–1918) took charge as the HUS's Secretary.[74]

The Second Fundraising Campaign

Malaviya began what me may identify as the second phase of his fundraising campaign for the Hindu University after constituting the HUS. This time, for the most part, the Maharaja of Darbhanga, kept his company and the fundraising effort, to an extent, deliberately focused on the princely states.

Malaviya, it seems, visited the Unnao, Sitapur, and Etawah districts of UP to seek donations for the Hindu University[75] in the end days of November (we do not have the exact dates for these trips, the conjecture is because these were undertaken after the HUS was formed). He took a break from fundraising in the first week of December for a crucial appointment. Malaviya, Besant, and Rameshwar Singh travelled to Delhi at the head of a twenty-nine strong delegation and confabulated with Butler on 4 December 1911. The Viceroy's deputy for educational matters was in the city for the grand durbar. Butler received the trio and the party they were leading 'cordially'.

Malaviya, Besant, and Rameshwar Singh gave him a draft constitution of the Hindu University for 'consultation and advice'.[76] Butler, on his part, told them that any Act passed by the government to create this institution 'would not come into operation until the ... [HUS] had a sum of Rs Fifty lakhs in the Bank and was in a position to raise a further sum of one crore of rupees'.[77] As it appears, this requirement infused renewed urgency into the fundraising campaign and caused it to purposely approach royal donors for garnering large contributions. As a matter of fact, a formal decision to prioritize collections from the princely states was taken at a meeting conducted at the Central Hindu College, attended by the Maharajas of Darbhanga and Bikaner and 'some learned Pandits and leading citizens' on 31 January 1912.[78]

Malaviya and Rameshwar Singh visited Ajmer to raise funds for the Hindu University on 13 May. They travelled to Moradabad and Bareilly on 2 and 4 June, respectively.[79] On 1 July, Rameshwar Singh was granted an audience with the ruler of Jammu and Kashmir and received from him a 'gift' of 'Rs. 3,50,000/-' for the Hindu University. Maharaja Hari Singh (1895–1961) also announced a grant 'forever' from the State Treasury of 'Rs. 1000-/ a month' for the institution.[80] Many of his high-ranking officials and prominent subjects made their own financial contributions for the cause of the Hindu University.[81]

In all, as we see, Rameshwar Singh's objective in travelling to Jammu and Kashmir was very well fulfilled. He rejoined Malaviya in Ambala where they addressed a public meeting at the Victoria Memorial Hall. 'About Rs 20,000/- were subscribed' in the event.[82] They went to Saharanpur the next day. Lucknow figured on their itinerary on 19 July. On 21 July, Malaviya and Rameshwar Singh visited Rai Bareilly.[83] On 26 August, the former waited on the Maharana of Udaipur who pledged Rs 1 lakh for the Hindu University.[84] Next, Malaviya spent 2–3 September in the princely state of Kota, where the Maharao personally presented him with a purse of Rs 1 lakh.[85]

After a few months' break, on 22 January 1913, Malaviya resumed his fundraising campaign at Allahabad. From there, accompanied by Rameshwar Singh and a small delegation, he went to Nabha, another princely state, and secured a contribution of Rs 1 lakh from the ruler.[86] The two, and the three other gentlemen comprising the delegation, next spent three days, 3–5 February in the Jodhpur State. Its Council of Regency, under the Presidency of Maharaja Pratap Singh (1845–1922), 'sanctioned a subscription of two lacs to the funds of the University and an annual endowment of Rs 24,000 for a chair of Technology to be called the Jodhpur Hardinge chair, subject to the concurrence of Lord Hardinge',[87] the Viceroy (1858–1944). Malaviya and Rameshwar Singh addressed a public meeting on the last day of their visit to the Jodhpur State and raised subscriptions for the Hindu University.[88]

On 15 February, they visited Udaipur with their companions and thanked the Maharana for Rs 5 lakh he had contributed on a prior date (we do not know when this was). The party reached Indore on 18 February. Their next stop was Bombay, where a grand reception was given in their honour on 21 February. Interestingly, we discover that it was organized by a committee headed by the Agha Khan (the spiritual head of the Ismaili Shia community), 'who had been very friendly to the [Hindu] university scheme from the start'. Later, Malaviya and the Maharaja of Darbhanga addressed a public meeting in the coastal city, where a total sum of Rs 2 lakh was pledged for the Hindu University. A committee was formed and entrusted with collecting this amount. The fundraising campaign came to an abrupt halt in Bombay when Malaviya fell ill and left for the hills to recuperate.[89]

The Banaras Hindu University Is Born

A total of Rs 21,37,539 had been by now collected for the Hindu University, while a further Rs 80 lakh had been subscribed or pledged.[90] Although the amount raised was still far from the Rs 50 lakh stipulated by Butler before the institution could become operational, Rameshwar Singh wrote to him to secure a legislation for the Hindu University. Addressing a letter to the colonial in charge of education on 28 April, he provided a detailed account of the funds brought in for the institution. He also informed Butler about the sums pledged by the Maharajas of Gwalior, Alwar, Bikanir [sic.], Nabha, Banaras, and Jodhpur totalling Rs 11 lakh. To this amount he added the Rs 3 lakh, the unpaid portion of his own donation for the Hindu University and arrived at a sum of Rs 14 lakh. Rameshwar Singh assured Butler that this amount would be paid for the Hindu University 'as soon as the Government desire[d]'.[91] 'In addition,' the Maharaja of Darbhanga wrote:

> [T]he Maharaja of Cossimbazar [sic] ... [was] transferring property in trust of the value of one lakh ... [and it] would bring Rs 3,500 a year and Babu Rajendra Kishore Roy Chaudhry, who ... [was] also a donor of one lakh, ... [was] similarly transferring property which would bring ... [them] Rs 3,500 a year more net.[92]

Rameshwar Singh was counting on several subscriptions of 'Rs 50,000 and above', which he estimated would total Rs 6.65 lakh. As he reckoned, there was going to be 'no difficulty whatsoever in collecting these'.[93] The Maharaja of Darbhanga also drew Butler's attention to the 'grants in perpetuity' pledged by the Maharajas of Jodhpur (Rs 24,000), Jammu and Kashmir (Rs 12,000), and Bikanir (Rs 12,000), amounting to Rs 48,000 annually. When 'capitalized at the rate of 3.5 per cent', he calculated, these 'allowances' came 'to about 14 lakhs in value'.[94] Finally, Rameshwar Singh factored in 'the value of the Central Hindu College ... [which had been] put down at about Rs 14 lakhs'. He, therefore, thought that 'more than the amount required' had been raised and that they were 'in a position to ask the Government to be so good as to take into consideration the legislation necessary for bringing the [Hindu] University into existence'.[95]

Butler, it appears, mulled over Rameshwar Singh's letter and, consequently, took a while to get back to him. In his reply dated 2 June, he demanded that the following conditions are fulfilled before the Government would consider legislating for the Hindu University:

1) That a suitable site be provided;
2) That the Central Hindu College be transferred to the University;
3) That the sum of 50 lakhs be collected. In this amount may be included the capitalized value of the property … [to be transferred by the Maharaja of Cossimbazar [sic] and Babu Rajendra Kishore Roy Chaudhry] and the perpetual grants … [by the Maharajas of Jodhpur, Jammu and Kashmir, Bikanir] … provided the documentary title is satisfactory in the case of the latter and possession of the property has been made over in the case of the former
4) That the constitution of the University [should] proceed on lines to be indicated to you hereafter;
5) That a committee appointed for the purpose [should] report that the Central Hindu College is fit to be developed into a residential and teaching University.[96]

The HUS took slightly more than a year to meet Butler's demand regarding a suitable site for the Hindu University. As we find, it began by shortlisting a few possible locations for the campus in Banaras: Nagwa, the Rajghat plateau, Kamachchha (where the Central Hindu College was situated), Sarnath, and Harahua near Shivpur. Ultimately, Nagwa was found to be the most suitable. The Rajghat plateau was a small area, Kamachchha was distant from the Ganga River and similarly cramped, while Harahua was far both from the riverfront and Banaras city. The grounds at Sarnath were large enough at 1,120 acres but Nagwa was favoured because it was cheap and close to the city.

The site was inspected by Butler and Henry Sharp, Educational Commissioner for the Government of India, on 22 July 1914. It was approved after they had a discussion with Rameshwar Singh, Malaviya, and Sundar Lal.[97] Several orthodox Hindus, however, were not pleased with the Hindu University's campus being built at Nagwa. This was because, in their view, the site fell outside the sacred precincts of Banaras. The orthodox objection to Nagwa was competently answered by a certain Bhagwan Das with 'a learned contribution in the press'. He marshalled the requisite facts to prove that the chosen site was not, after all, outside the limits of the holy city. Later, when the campus became operational in 1916, the HUS would again placate the orthodox by not enclosing the Panch Kroshi road. The reason being that, once again, they regarded it to be beyond the pales of Banaras.[98]

Prior to the finalization of a site for the campus, the formalities regarding the transfer of the Central Hindu College to the Hindu University had been completed on 19 April. The formal handover of the institution to Sundar Lal took place in September. Much to the disappointment of Besant, its Theosophist professors were not retained.[99] This was yet again due to the orthodox lobby's discomfort with them. Interestingly, the government did not insist on their retention either,[100] although Butler had wanted the Hindu University to have an 'adequate European staff'. Malaviya was also reluctant to include the trustees of the Central Hindu College in the governing bodies of the Hindu University.[101] Presumably, this too was due to the tinge of Theosophy borne by the institution.

Fulfilling the third condition set by Butler took some work on the part of Malaviya. As far as we gather, there was no issue concerning the properties transferred and perpetual grants made to the Hindu University (since nothing to the effect is mentioned anywhere). However, about 38,000 letters were dispatched from the HUS's Allahabad office to realize the sums subscribed for the Hindu University. Malaviya also had to tour several towns and cities he had previously visited during the fundraising campaigns to collect the monies committed to the institution. In this way, he finally managed to put together the stipulated Rs 50 lakh by the beginning of 1915.[102]

Some basics of the Hindu University's constitution, as they might be termed, meanwhile, were being determined. To begin with, Butler enjoined that it may not affiliate colleges outside Banaras (apparently overruling the draft constitution he had been presented with by Malaviya, Besant, and Rameshwar Singh). Apropos its name, at one stage he conveyed to the Maharaja of Darbhanga that the Secretary of State wished the institution to be called the 'University of Benares' (seemingly on account of being favourably disposed towards Besant's one-time proposal).[103]

Butler did not relent on the first point despite the ardent protestations of Rameshwar Singh. However, he seems to have seen logic in the latter's plea that, being located in Banaras, 'the sacred city of the Hindus, the association of the word *Hindu* in … [the university's] name … [would] not only satisfy a much-cherished sentiment, but … also indicate and point out that it … [is] for the benefit of the entire Hindu community of India'.[104] Subsequently, in December 1914, Butler approved the name 'Banaras Hindu University' to 'meet the sentiment of the subscribers'. However, he laid down that there would be no religious test at the institution, and it would be 'open to students of all denominations as well as to Hindus'. He also stipulated that 'Hindu theological teaching and observances ... [would] not be compulsory for any but Hindus' at BHU.[105]

Butler, due to some reason, did not enforce the condition that a committee would examine the Central Hindu College's suitability to be developed as a residential and teaching university (in other words, to be BHU's kernel). The other requirements set by him fulfilled, and an institutional constitution delineated in its rudiments, he introduced the 'Banaras Hindu University Bill' in the Imperial Legislative Council on 22 March 1915. Butler was quite effusive in describing the institution that was being created. His colleagues in the house, he said, were

> watching ... the birth of a new and, many hope, a better type of university in India. The main features of this university which distinguish it from existing universities ... [are] first, that it ... [is] a teaching and residential university, secondly, that while it ... [is] open to all castes and creeds it ... [insists] upon religious instruction for Hindus, and, thirdly, that it ... [would] be conducted and managed by the Hindu community and almost entirely by non-officials.[106]

Butler termed BHU an 'all-India university' and announced that it was commencing 'with 'five faculties, Arts, Science, Law, Oriental Studies and Theology'[107] (Malaviya's vision, as we see, stood much modified). Then he proceeded to flesh out the institution's constitution in the way of some vital details. The Governor-General, Butler revealed, was BHU's 'Lord Rector', and the Lieutenant Governor of the United Provinces was its 'Visitor'. Alongside, BHU would have 'Patrons, Vice Patrons and Rectors'. The university would be run by four bodies: namely, Senate, Syndicate, Court, and Council. All academic matters were to form the Senate's purview. It would comprise '(a) The Chancellor, the Pro-Chancellor, the Vice-Chancellor for the time being; (b) The University Professors; (c) The Principals or heads of constituent colleges of the University'.

Besides, the Senate would include five members 'elected by the Court', five 'representatives of Hindu religion and Sanskrit learning to be elected by … [itself]', and five more members 'nominated by the Visitor'. The Syndicate, Butler clarified,

> [would] consist of the Vice-Chancellor, Pro-Vice-Chancellor and fifteen members of whom not ten shall be University Professors or principals and professors of constituent colleges. The object aimed at … [was] to secure that purely academic matters should be decided by a body mainly expert while the Government (sic.) and the supervision of the University rests with the Court and the Council.

The Senate was represented on the Council (whose full composition Butler did not reveal) so that the 'academic view may always be before it'. The Court (also not described in terms of membership) was meant to 'elect … [BHU's] Chancellor, Vice-Chancellor, and Pro-Chancellor'. These 'officers' were to be 'scheduled' in the 'first instance', (that is, they would be appointed without an election at the time of the university becoming operational). The Vice-Chancellor would be 'ex-officio Chairman of the Council, the Senate and the Syndicate'. Further, he would 'be the Chief Executive officer of the University'.[108] BHU would, 'through the Council and the Board of Appointments appoint its own professors and staff and have entire control over them'.[109] The university was, in this way, given some significant autonomy.

The foregoing constitution, Butler declared was not 'ill-liberal' [sic] in any form. Instead, he said, 'It ... [was] far more liberal than the constitution [sic.] of existing universities.' The 'Government,' Butler thought, had 'trusted' the HUS, and given it a 'large autonomy' leaving for itself 'only the necessary power of intervention if things go wrong'.[110]

The colonial in charge of education, it appears, was aware of the disappointment he had caused by disallowing BHU from affiliating colleges outside Banaras. Butler, therefore, dwelt on its national scope to underline that it was still an 'all-India university'. The institution, he said, would

> accept for admission to its courses all candidates from schools at present recognized by an existing university or by a local Government or by a Durbar, who have passed the matriculation examination of such university or obtained a recognized school-leaving certificate.[111]

BHU, resultantly, was 'open to students from every province and Native State in India'.[112] Also, Butler pointed out, its

> governing body ... [was] recruited from the length and breadth of India. It ... [would] send forth its alumni to every quarter of India. It ... [would] number among its patrons Governors and heads of Provinces, Ruling Chiefs and other eminent benefactors in all parts of India.[113]

BHU, in other words, was based in Banaras, but not confined to it in terms of outreach.

Presently it was Malaviya's turn to speak. He began by emphasizing that there was nothing communal or parochial about BHU despite it being a denominational university. 'It ... [would] not promote narrow sectarianism,' Malaviya announced, 'but a broad liberation of mind and a religious spirit ... [building] brotherly feeling between man and man.' The religious influence, he averred, 'is ever ennobling'. Hence, Malaviya opined that 'where the true religious spirit is inculcated, there must be an elevated feeling of humility'. It also, he believed, imparted love of God which, in turn, cultivated 'greater love and less hatred of man'. Therefore, Malaviya dismissed apprehensions about religious instruction being compulsory at BHU (for Hindu students). He assured his fellow legislators that 'It... [would] lead to nothing but good'.[114]

Further, Malaviya pointed out, mandatory religious instruction at BHU would motivate 'religious minded Hindu donors' to contribute to the institution.[115] He also sought to allay worries, in case there were any, as to how this instruction would deal with the remarkable diversity of beliefs and practices among Hindus. It would, Malaviya said, be such as to 'be acceptable to all sections of the Hindu community'. BHU, thus, would identify with Hindu society at large and not a section or group thereof.

However, Malaviya declared, its denominational identity notwithstanding, professors at the institution would not be disqualified during selection on grounds of religion. He, in other words, implied that it was not necessary to be a Hindu to teach at BHU. The university was also, Malaviya told the house, open to students of every 'creed' and 'class'. When it came to its administration, the membership of the Senate was open to non-Hindus (although the Court was to be exclusively Hindu).[116] BHU, thus, was a Hindu institution in essence, but it was also tolerant and accepting in its outlook.

The Banaras Hindu University Bill was eventually passed by the Imperial Legislative Council after slightly more than six months, on 1 October 1915.[117] British-ruled India, in this way, had its first denominational university. It was also its first university established entirely through private initiative. In both respects, BHU was a remarkable achievement and a unique intervention in colonial higher education.

4

BHU: The Making of an Institution (1916–47)

A Beginning Marred by Controversy

The foundation stone of BHU was originally meant to be laid on 8 February 1916. Astrologers had recommended the date to the HUS since it was Basant Panchami, when Devi Saraswati, the presiding deity of arts and learning, would be worshipped. However, the ceremony had to be brought forward and conducted on 4 February. This was because the Viceroy, Lord Hardinge (1858–1944), whom the HUS had invited as chief guest, was unavailable on 8 February due to prior engagements.

A nineteen-member committee headed by Malaviya made the necessary preparations for the big day. It deliberated a lot along the way holding, as we learn, a total of twenty-two meetings. The committee received the 'active cooperation' of the colonial authorities. James Meston (1865–1943), the Lieutenant-Governor of the United Provinces of Agra and Oudh (as the NWP&O was renamed in 1902), personally visited Banaras to take stock of the arrangements. In an apparent bid to ensure that nothing was lacking, he also put the services of the province's Public Works Department at the disposal of BHU.[1]

The committee selected a site along the *pucca* (metaled) road to the Nagwa ghat for the foundation stone-laying ceremony. This was an 'open piece of ground, five or six furlongs from the stream of the Ganga opposite Ramnagar fort, the residence of the Maharaja of Banaras'.[2] As the appointed day approached, the ceremony was rehearsed thrice.[3] Malaviya and his team were obviously anxious to avoid any lapse in protocol with the Viceroy in attendance.

Lord Hardinge disembarked at Banaras railway station at 10:30 a.m. on 4 February. He was received by Rameshwar Singh, Meston, some local officials, and Malaviya, along with the HUS. Proceeding first to the palace of the Maharaja of Banaras, the Viceroy reached the site of the foundation stone-laying ceremony at 12:30 p.m.[4] He was seated on a dais in an enormous pandal.[5] Rulers of several princely states, high-ranking colonial officials, and members of the HUS sat on the Viceroy's either side.[6] A conspicuous absence was Butler's. He had expressed his inability to attend (without citing a reason) in a telegram addressed to Rameshwar Singh on 2 February.[7] On the other hand, although in attendance, Besant was not seated on the dais with the Viceroy. We are told that she was 'kept studiously in the background at this function'.[8] This was due to her involvement in the Home Rule Movement at the time and the speeches criticizing the government she was delivering. Besant thus received a bit of a snub at the foundation stone-laying ceremony, her immense contribution to the cause of BHU notwithstanding. The HUS found it expedient to not offend the Viceroy in any manner.

Twelve 'little girls from the Central Hindu College Girls' School … chanted a short Sanskrit invocation, first to Ganapati and then to Goddess Saraswati', and provided a 'very fitting opening to the ceremony'. Then, 'the great Pandit, Mahamahopadhyaya Shiva Kumar Shastri … came forward and uttered svastivachana slokas, words of prayer for the blessing of God upon the work to be performed'. After this, Rameshwar Singh rose to read out a welcome address for the Viceroy. He expressed the 'fervent gratitude' of the HUS that Lord Hardinge had accepted the invitation to preside over the ceremony. The Maharaja of Darbhanga also thanked him for the 'generous support and encouragement' that had 'contributed so much to the realization of the earnest hopes and aspirations of Hindu India'.[9] Then, after relating the history of the movement for a Hindu university,[10] he dwelt on the reasons that necessitated its establishment. He said,

> It is impossible to recall the state of education which existed in India at the start of British rule and compare it with the stage it has now reached, without a sense of deep gratitude to the Government which has brought about this momentous change. Great also is our indebtedness to the existing Universities which have contributed in so large a measure to the diffusion of higher education among our people. But these universities are, at present, mainly examining bodies, and there is an ever growing consensus of opinion that those Universities also can discharge their high functions and fulfill their mission which teach as well as examine, which impart not only literary but also scientific and technical education combined with research, and which mould the character of their alumni by helping them to live their academic life in healthy environments, under the personal influence and loving care of good and capable teachers.[11]

Rameshwar Singh, in other words, acknowledged the benefits of the colonial framework of higher education while pointing out what he thought was lacking in it. BHU had been established to address and mitigate this lack with a unique and original vision. An institution like BHU was also required, the Maharaja of Darbhanga declared, to preserve the ancient 'culture and civilization' the Hindus were inheritors to. They wished, he said, to have 'a central educational institution of … [their] own, to preserve and promote … [their] distinctive civilization and culture, and to instruct … [their] youth in the sacred precepts of … [their] religion'. Brought up thus in their 'traditions and culture', Rameshwar Singh assured the Viceroy, Hindu youth would become 'men of vigorous intellects and high character, who love their Motherland, are loyal to the King, and are in every way fit to be useful members of the community and worthy citizens of a great empire'.[12] The Maharaja of Darbhanga, as it were, made BHU's additional raison d'être supplying competent, moral, and socially and culturally rooted graduates who would be, in the final analysis, loyal to the British sovereign and the British empire.

His words do somewhat discomfit us over more than a century. Nevertheless, we ought to see this part of Rameshwar Singh's address as an attempt to ensure that the nascent institution is in the good graces of the colonial authorities and receives their support. As we shall discover subsequently, BHU turned out to be anything but a hub of king and empire loyalists.

Presently, it was the Viceroy's turn to reply. He began by marvelling at the 'distinguished gathering', which included the 'Governor of Bengal, a constellation of Lieutenant Governors, a veritable galaxy of ruling princes, and so much of the flower of India's intellect'.[13] Lord Hardinge termed the occasion as one of 'deep significance', betokening 'a new departure in the history of education in India'.[14] BHU's constitution, he noted, made it 'a teaching and residential, as contrasted with an affiliating and examining, university'. The Viceroy observed that the 'prototype' of this setup could be 'dimly discerned in the far distant past' of India when students 'gathered round such great teachers as Vashishtha and Gautama'. According to him,

> [T]he whole Indian idea of education ... [was] wrapped up in the conception of a group of pupils surrounding their "guru" in loving reverence and not only imbibing the words of wisdom that fall from his lips, but also looking up to him for guidance in religion and morality and moulding their character in accordance with his precept and example.

Apparently, since BHU was realizing this idea, Lord Hardinge found it worthy of the government's consistent support.[15]

The Viceroy also wholeheartedly countenanced the denominational character of the institution. He found 'education without religion ... [to be] of little worth'. Lord Hardinge hoped that BHU would

> in the not too far distant future ... [preserve and foster] all that is best in Hindu ideals of life and thought; all that is noblest of Hindu religion and tradition, culture and civilization, and grafted upon that tree, healthy and strong in its own natural soil ... [would] grow in it and of it, all that is good and great of Western science, industry and art, so that ... young men may go forth, not only inspired with pure and noble ideals, but also equipped for

> the development of their mother country along the more material lines of progress and prosperity.[16]

The Viceroy envisaged BHU perpetuating the finest aspects of Hinduism and adopting what was worthy in Western learning. The Indian founders of the institution, as well as its foremost colonial enabler, shared the same vision for it.

Lord Hardinge left for Ramnagar to partake in a luncheon hosted by the Maharaja of Banaras after laying the foundation stone.[17] The ceremony itself, however, did not conclude. In fact, it continued for the next four days (until Basant Panchami) with cricket matches and pujas. Several eminent speakers also delivered addresses over this duration.[18]

For instance, Dr J.C. Bose (1858–1937) gave a lecture titled 'From the Voiced to the Unvoiced' on 6 February.[19] One issue he considered was the 'comparative want of success in scientific investigation in India'. Bose identified 'the want of the due recognition of the experimental side' as the reason behind this situation. However, he felt that India was otherwise 'pre-eminently fitted for [scientific] investigation'. This was because, in his view, 'an Indian enquirer had not only a burning imagination which could extort truth out of a mass of apparently disconnected facts, but also the habit of meditation, whereby the mental vision is kept clear and steady'.[20] Bose, thus, was quite optimistic that India was well poised for achievements in the field of scientific investigation, on account of its unique talents, the relative neglect of hands-on inquiries through experimentation notwithstanding.

Besant spoke on the theme 'The University as a Builder of Character'[21] on the same day as Bose. She eloquently reflected on the ideals that BHU had been brought forth to pursue. 'The first great ideal of the Hindu University', as seen by this naturalized Indian and Hindu, was 'to take up the Hindu culture, and enrich it, but not supplant it, with all that the other civilizations can give'. She, as we see it, visualized BHU as a conduit through which propitious and invigorating influences would be absorbed into Hindu culture. The second ideal Besant identified for the institution was a love of knowledge 'for knowledge's sake'. This is since, in her understanding, Hindus did not take a purely utilitarian view of knowledge. As Besant put it, 'To a Hindu, to think of knowledge as a source of gain ... [is] sacrilege.'[22] She wanted BHU, in this way, to live up to a core Hindu ethos.

The great Sanskrit scholar Mahamahopadhyaya Pandit Hara Prasad Shastri's (1853–1931) turn to speak was on 7 February. He lectured on the 'Value of Sanskrit Education.'[23] The renowned physicist C.V. Raman (1880–1970) spoke on 'Some New Paths in Physics'[24] the following day. He shared an account of 'his own researches in Physics, whereby he discovered some new paths'. Raman also emphasized the study of mathematics (since, it seems, it was so integral to his field of inquiry) during his lecture. Terming mathematics the 'science of sciences', the savant traced its 'early history in India to the days of Aryabhatta'. India, he said, need not 'look to foreign countries for inspiration', because 'it was in India that numerical figures were invented, and ... the decimal system of notation originated'. Raman, thus, urged the audience to 'look to the glorious past of ... [their] own country'.[25]

Nationalist in tone as they were (in one way or another), the foregoing lectures were much appreciated. A jarring note was, however, struck by the address of South Africa-returned lawyer and political activist Mohandas

Karamchand Gandhi. It stirred controversy and piqued many in the audience by being overly political, hectoring, and agitational. Gandhi was the last to speak on 6 February. His rambling, unstructured talk, reproduced in slightly divergent versions in the *Leader* and *Abhyudaya* newspapers (which agreed on its main points),[26] was without an overarching theme or title.[27] Considering the occasion, it was also quite out of place. Unlike the other speakers, Gandhi did not discuss an academic topic. Neither did he comment on BHU's mission or objectives. He, instead, began by bemoaning the 'awfully insanitary condition of the sacred city of Banaras'. Gandhi asked the audience how they might be able to govern themselves (perhaps, he had the demand for Home Rule in mind) if they are unable to keep even the 'holy temple' of Vishwanath clean. He had scant expectations from Indian self-government when even temples in India were 'not models of roominess and cleanliness'. Hereon, he moved to another issue altogether without a preamble of any sort. Speaking in English, 'He confessed to a sense of shame that he had to address an Indian audience in a foreign language and regretted that everybody else had done the same'.[28] Next, Gandhi decried the resort to arms to secure national independence. He termed this, as he put it, 'cult of terrorism and secret assassination … cowardly', and urged the audience to shun it. Gandhi's disapproving gaze then turned towards the 'pomp and jewellery displayed by the ruling princes which contrasted with the grinding poverty of their people'. He urged those present 'to adopt plain living so as to be able to serve the people'. Winding up, Gandhi 'expressed his strong disapproval of the heavy security arrangements made for the Viceroy which had filled … [Banaras] with secret service men'. His concluding, rather scandalous remark, allegedly was, 'Lord Hardinge should have chosen rather to be shot than subject the people to such humiliation.'[29]

Gandhi's seeming lack of propriety left several important people in the audience quite aghast. At one point, Besant stood up to remind him that he was addressing 'a body of impressionable young men'.[30] This was probably during his ill-mannered and uncalled-for allusion to the resplendence of the royal attendees and the Viceroy's security protocol. The Commissioner of the Banaras Division, a certain Mr Hopkins, walked out while Gandhi was speaking. So did many others. Even Rameshwar Singh, the Chair for Gandhi's talk, rose and left abruptly as per 'one account'.[31]

Gandhi's peroration predictably angered the colonial officials and caused an uproar in a section of the press (presumably the loyalist English-language periodicals). Nevertheless, the topmost authority in the province, Lieutenant-Governor Meston, chose to show restraint and decided that 'no action should be taken in connection with the [foundation stone-laying] ceremony'. This was apparently because he did not wish to 'leave a stain' on its record. The provincial government, however, decided to monitor Gandhi's 'future visits' (within its jurisdiction) and take steps to 'prevent him from becoming publicly intoxicated by his own verbosity'.[32] It also noted 'the glaring failure of the Maharaja of Darbhanga to keep the speaker within proper limits, in [the] face of an excited crowd of students'.[33] Gandhi's irresponsible conduct at the foundation stone-laying ceremony thus caused one of the most important partisans of BHU to suffer the indignity of an official reprimand. But for the Lieutenant-Governor's maturity, Gandhi would have brought official ire upon the nascent institution too. As we shall see subsequently, this would not be the only instance of Gandhi making himself something of an annoyance for BHU.

Travails of a Fledgling Institution

Appointing BHU's first Chancellor, Pro-Chancellor, and Vice-Chancellor was the government's prerogative. However, it acted according to the suggestions of Malaviya when filling the first two positions. He, respectively, recommended Maharaja Madhav Rao Scindia of Gwalior (1876–1925) for Chancellor and Maharaja Krishna Raja Wadiyar of Mysore (1884–1940) for Pro-Chancellor after waiting upon them and obtaining their consent. Apparently, Malaviya preferred royalty in a couple of topmost administrative positions at BHU on account of two considerations. They, he believed, would help attract funds to the institution and rally the sentiments of Hindu society in its favour. For the post of Vice-Chancellor, Malaviya suggested the name of Sir Gooroo Das Banerji (1844–1918), a former judge of the Calcutta High Court and a highly respected figure. However, the colonial authorities were wary of his sympathies for the armed revolutionaries. The government, thus, preferred to appoint Sundar Lal to the office instead.[34]

As it turned out, the early years of BHU were marked by a degree of instability, with the occupants of its top administrative offices changing rather rapidly. Sundar Lal did not continue in his position long enough to steady the institution and guide it through its infancy. Assuming charge on 1 April 1916, he suddenly passed away on 13 February 1918. His stint as the Vice-Chancellor, resultantly, was not even properly two years long.

Malaviya was requested to take up the role by the university Court, but he declined (seemingly in view of his political commitments). Subsequently, he proposed Sir P.S. Sivaswamy Aiyar (1864–1946), the Vice-Chancellor of Madras University, as Sundar Lal's successor. The Court complied and elected him to the position. Aiyar, however, was unable or unwilling to relocate from Madras (now Chennai) to Banaras due to his professional commitments at Madras University and his involvement in public life of the Madras Presidency. The most he could commit to was spending a total of ninety days, or about three months, annually at BHU, that too not at a stretch. He would be on campus from ten to fifteen days to about a month at a time. Aiyar, thus, was largely an absentee Vice-Chancellor. Nevertheless, being an experienced administrator, he still discharged his office competently for as long as he occupied it. Unfortunately, Aiyar relinquished the Vice-Chancellorship all of a sudden in May 1919, barely a year after he had assumed it.[35] Besant would later allege that he chose to resign because certain members of the Court insisted on speaking in Hindi during meetings. This greatly inconvenienced Aiyar since he was completely ignorant of the language.[36] It is quite likely that the Court was not unanimously in favour of an 'outsider' from another province becoming the Vice-Chancellor of BHU. Some of the members, consequently, ganged up on Aiyar and got rid of him. At the same time, his resignation could be due to disagreements with Malaviya over some major issues. For instance, Aiyar wanted the university to remain a non-affiliating, unitary entity. On the other hand, Malaviya was keen on incorporating the Government Sanskrit College into BHU and affiliate institutions imparting Sanskrit learning all over the country. Secondly, unlike Malaviya, Aiyar did not want only Brahmin faculty to provide religious instruction at BHU.[37]

At the time of Aiyar's resignation, Malaviya was the university's Pro-Vice-Chancellor. The first occupant of the office was Aditya Ram Bhattacharya, his teacher from college days. After Sundar Lal's demise, the burden of running BHU chiefly fell on Bhattacharya's shoulders. A man of advanced years, he struggled to cope and eventually resigned in 1918. Bhattacharya was succeeded by Gnanendranath Chakravarty. With Aiyar mostly away, he was generally in charge of decision-making and felt it necessary to ensure continuity of policies at BHU. Chakravarty thus asked the Court to unanimously grant him a tenure of three years. When the court failed to reach a consensus on this matter, he resigned. Subsequently, Malaviya consented to take Chakravarty's place at the Court's request.[38] This was in early 1919. In the aftermath of Aiyar's departure, in November that year, the Court successfully persuaded Malaviya to assume the Vice-Chancellor's office. He went on to occupy this position for a full two decades, deftly steering BHU through crises and providing it the much-required stability of leadership. Chakravarty returned as the Pro-Vice-Chancellor after Malaviya vacated the position. His stint, however, turned out to be brief as he left in April 1920 to become the Vice-Chancellor of the newly established Lucknow University. Prof. A.B. Dhruva of the Gujarat College now took charge in Chakravarty's stead. He turned out to be a most able deputy to Malaviya. Dhruva also nearly matched his longevity in office. He served as the Pro-Vice-Chancellor for a decade and a half before eventually quitting in 1936.[39]

Financial woes plagued BHU for a long time. To start with, the institution's monetary resources were strained by Malaviya's grand construction plans for the Nagwa campus. By 1920, the situation was so acute that Malaviya had to embark on a fundraising campaign with a team of fourteen. The gentlemen had a reasonably successful tour. A trip to Bombay, for instance, yielded Rs 25 lakh in promised sums.[40] Over the next two years, Malaviya mitigated BHU's financial struggles by raising considerable donations. Resultantly, the university not just remained solvent, but even managed to float courses in electrical and mechanical engineering and 'some branches' of technology. This was during the Non-Cooperation Movement when Malaviya had joined in the boycott of the legislatures. He, thus, had enough time to raise monies for BHU.[41]

As Malaviya resumed his usual political activities after the Non-Cooperation Movement, BHU's financial condition became rather desperate. Without his involvement, the university could raise a mere Rs 1.04 lakh in donations in the year 1923–24. By 1925, it had accumulated (by the standards of the days) a colossal debt of Rs 17.25 lakh. Consequently, Dhruva had to appoint a couple of committees to recommend economizing means. Nevertheless, the grim financial situation did not let up. A collection campaign launched by BHU in 1926 abjectly failed in Malaviya's absence.

Next, the university adopted some measures to increase its earnings. It raised the tuition fees and imposed a levy of Rs 8 per annum on students for medicines. The medicine levy was foisted on the employees too at the annual rates of Rs 10 and Rs 20 per annum respectively on monthly salaries of Rs 500 and above. The rise in income achieved through these means, however, was modest and BHU's budget shortfall continued.

An appeal to the government for funds resulted in it increasing its annual grant to the university from Rs 1 lakh to Rs 1.25 lakh. The government also agreed to release Rs 5 lakh to BHU in two instalments to help it service its debt. The first instalment of Rs 2 lakh was provided in 1926. When it came to the remaining amount, the government made its release conditional on the university reducing its debt by more than Rs 2 lakh by May 1927. As we gather, BHU did not even attempt to meet this condition. The university, instead, (apparently without success) requested that its annual governmental grant be increased to Rs 2 lakh and it is given a non-recurring grant of Rs 20 lakh (inclusive of Rs 5 lakh already sanctioned) for debt servicing.[42]

BHU's financial situation somewhat looked up in 1927 with a reasonably successful collection campaign. It brought in more than Rs 7 lakh in two phases. Malaviya also elicited considerable financial contributions from the princely states of Rajputana and Central India in December that year. The Maharaja of Bikaner, for instance, gave Rs 50,000, while the potentates of Kota and Jodhpur donated Rs 1 lakh and Rs 2 lakh, respectively. The Sardars (hereditary feudal chiefs) of the Gwalior State collectively subscribed Rs 43,000 for BHU. By June 1928, the university had reduced its debt to Rs 12.5 lakh.[43]

Probably feeling optimistic due to the inflow of funds, Malaviya went the whole hog in August and issued a lengthy public appeal to raise Rs 1 crore for BHU. Titled the 'Appeal for a Second Crore', this pamphlet explained that the 'first crore of rupees subscribed and paid up [for BHU] … [had] been exhausted nearly half of it being kept as permanent endowment [sic]'. Hence, the appeal was being issued for 'a second crore'.[44] The candidly worded text described the current financial circumstances of the university in the following terms:

> The expenditure necessary efficiently to carry on the work of the existing Faculties is nearly twelve lakhs, but the annual income of the University is less than seven lakhs. It needs therefore an addition of 5 lakhs a year to its annual income … [BHU is] very grateful that the Government of India have, in response to … [its] appeal, recently raised their annual grant from 1.25 lakhs to Rs 3 lakhs a year. But … [BHU] still … [needs] Rs 3 lakhs a year more to balance … [its] budget and to effect [sic] some very necessary improvements.[45]

The 'Appeal for a Second Crore' also explained why BHU's revenues from tuition fees were meagre:

> Our income from fees is … comparatively small for the reasons that (a) no tuition fee is charged from any student of Theology, of Oriental Learning and of Ayurveda and in the Teachers' Training College, and the Women's College; (b) 10 per cent of the students of all other colleges, except the Law College, are exempt from the payment of the tuition fee, and another 10 per cent from payment of half the fee, (c) our fees are lower than those charged in any other university in British India.[46]

Further, the pamphlet assured prospective donors that BHU pursues the best academic standards, and that its staff take little or nothing in the way of salaries, being motivated by the spirit of service instead of pecuniary concerns. At the same time, it observed that the university might require to spend more on salaries hereafter:

> [T]he number and salaries of ... [BHU's] staff are necessarily lower than those in other universities. Yet by strenuous labor the standards of teaching and examination have been maintained at quite a high level. The University is largely being helped by the principle of self-sacrifice among its workers. Its Vice-Chancellor has always been an unpaid officer, so also the Pro-Vice-Chancellor, and the Principal of the College of Theology. A number of other worthy members of the academic and administrative staff have served the University as Honorary workers for varying periods. But some of these posts will have to be filled by full time salaried workers in the future.[47]

The 'Appeal for a Second Crore' urged 'every Hindu prince and peasant to contribute his or her quota' to build up BHU, a 'national Temple of Learning', so that it continues its 'vigorous growth' and soon ranks 'among the best universities of the world'.[48]

Unfortunately, it seems, not enough Hindu princes and peasants came forward to respond to this earnest appeal. BHU, consequently, continued to be cash starved. By the end of 1928, its debt had again risen to Rs 16.36 lakh. A bit of relief came from the government in 1929 when it sanctioned the considerable sum of Rs 15 lakh to help BHU service its debt. It was to be released in three instalments. Additionally, the provincial administration chipped in with a recuring annual grant of Rs 50,000 for Ayurvedic Studies at the university. It also set aside a sum of Rs 3,000 per annum for free provision of medicines to poor BHU students. Chiefly on account of the

Rs 15 lakh grant, the institution came within spitting distance of attaining financial stability over the next three years. When BHU received the final instalment of this sum in 1932, its debt had come down to a manageable Rs 3.29 lakh.

Nevertheless, the university continued to be financially straitened. This was mainly due to two reasons. The great worldwide depression, ongoing since 1929, had dried up money in the economy. Both governmental and private contributions, as a result, were not forthcoming. In fact, the government was resorting to giving its employees salary cuts as an austerity measure. Second, once Malaviya involved himself in the Civil Disobedience Movement, the royal houses kept him at an arm's length and cut down on their largesse towards BHU (so as not to displease the colonial authorities). The university pulled through the next six years, it seems, mainly by suspending its expansion plans and the severest austerity measures; all unnecessary expenditures were given up.

BHU began to financially turn the corner after Sarvepalli Radhakrishnan (1888–1975) took charge as the Vice-Chancellor in 1939. He hired the honorary services of N.V. Raghavan, former Accountant General of British India, to manage the university's finances. Remarkably astute at balancing books, he managed to turn the recurring deficit in BHU's revenues into a modest surplus by the financial year 1940–41. This caused both the central and provincial governments to take a more charitable view of the institution. With the colonial authorities better disposed towards BHU, the native rulers too gradually gave up the frosty attitude they had come to adopt towards it. They now made generous donations to the institution as before.[49]

However, endowments from the princely states ceased yet again in 1942. This was on account of many BHU students joining the Quit India movement. The university, nevertheless, pulled through without suffering a serious budget shortfall. Very likely, this was due to the talents of Raghavan.

Academics at BHU

The first academic session at BHU commenced on 1 October 1917 in pursuance of a notification issued by the Viceroy.[50] The Nagwa campus not yet ready, the university functioned out of the premises of the Central Hindu College in these early days. It had only five faculties, or academic departments, for the time being. These were, Theology, Oriental Learning, Arts, Science (Pure and Applied), and Law.[51] In keeping with its founding vision, BHU sought to pedagogically meld Indian, or Hindu, and Western learning from the very outset. For instance, it was proposed (presumably by the Senate) that students be familiarized with Western discoveries and introduced to the use of telescope and other modern instruments in the astronomy course at the Faculty of Oriental Learning. A similar approach was suggested for teaching of mathematics and Sanskrit there. The Faculty of Oriental Learning sought to familiarize students with both the 'advances made in the mathematical science in the West' along with the 'ancient oriental systems' of mathematics. When it came to the Sanskrit course, it intended to make 'vernacular' instruction in modern liberal arts and humanities disciplines such as history and economics a part of it.[52]

Later, the Faculty of Oriental Learning would also try to combine the teaching of ayurveda with Western medicine.

The attempt was given up after BHU established the Faculty of Medicine and Surgery and began to teach courses in Western medicine.[53] Along with pedagogy, an epistemically hybrid approach informed the academic inquiries and writing undertaken at the university. Published to encourage research among faculty and students, *BHU Magazine*, for instance, would frequently carry papers on 'Indological' themes, that is, aspects of the civilizational heritage of India. Leah Renold, author of a brief study on BHU, observes that they displayed the tendency to present 'Hinduism in a modern light, using scientific terminology to support traditional ideas, or proving the antiquity of modern practices'.[54]

Teachers and students at BHU, in this way, worked to usher a 'Hindu renaissance'. But their approach towards this goal, as we observe, was somewhat non-traditional, or heterodox. It was guided by Western 'rationality' as they emphasized Hinduism's apparent compatibility with science and authenticated its contemporary orthopraxis through historical inquiries. To be sure, deeply orthodox cultural and religious positions, developed in the Sanskrit shastric or juristic framework alone, were articulated in *BHU Magazine* too. A case in point is the argument made by a student (in 1942) that 'the only people qualified to teach Hindu religion were Brahmans of unsullied character'.[55]

And then, *BHU Magazine* published papers on topics pertaining to geology and optics along with reports of important conferences and book reviews.[56] Thus, to borrow a term from the Russian philosopher Mikhail Bakhtin, the publication voiced a kind of 'heteroglossia',[57] a complex heterogeneity of opinions, concerns, and interests. It exemplified, we might say, the intellectual catholicity of BHU.

The two faculties (subsequently colleges) of Oriental Learning and Theology were, so to speak, the chief executors of the civilizational project undertaken by BHU, that is, preserving and imparting a distinctly Hindu learning. The former, for instance, taught the six philosophical systems, along with Kavya, Jyotisha, Ayurveda, Vyakarana, Agama, and classical languages such as Sanskrit, Prakrit, and Pali. The College of Oriental Learning was open to all Hindus, regardless of their jati identities,[58] although the learning it imparted had been often monopolized by Brahmins in traditional setups. It demonstrated, thus, a progressive bent and did not socially restrict itself from the point of view of enrolment. In the way of instruction, as we have seen, it gave adequate space to what it found relevant or necessary of Western knowledge and the technological means thereto. The college of Oriental Learning, consequently, despite the traditional knowledge it focused on, was to an extent an intellectually hybrid space. The College of Theology, however, was both orthodox and socially restricted. Only Brahmins could teach and learn there. It taught the Vedas and Karma-Kanda, or the performance of rituals.[59] The College of Theology, as we shall see, was made the exclusive preserve of Brahmans because it trained students to officiate as priests. Thus, BHU found it pointless to open it to other jati groups. A non-Brahmin, after all, would never be hired to discharge the priestly function by a patron (*jajman*) even if trained for it.

The Colleges of Oriental Learning and Theology were central to BHU's identity as a Hindu institution of higher learning. Ironically, however, they were the least preferred by students for enrolment. To give an example, there were a total of 3,411 scholars at BHU in the 1937-38 academic session.[60] Of these, not even 500 were being instructed at the Colleges of Oriental Learning and Theology. The former had 364 students, and the latter a mere 31.[61] Thus, even after a decade's existence the two colleges failed to attain significant traction in colonial higher education.

This was mainly due to the reason that their graduates struggled to secure jobs. The courses taught at the Colleges of Oriental Leaning and Theology produced pandits and priests who could not hope to be gainfully absorbed into the contemporary colonial administration and economy. Resultantly, learners preferred Western humanities and technical courses at BHU.[62] The university, on its part, tried its best to incentivize and popularize enrolment at the Colleges of Oriental Learning and Theology through the waiver of tuition fees and hostel charges.[63] These measures, nevertheless, were not very successful.

By 1921, the Nagwa campus had begun to take shape as a built landscape under the supervision of Frank Lishman (1869–1938), consulting architect to the government of the United Provinces, Rai Bahadur Ganga Ram (1851–1927), Honorary Chief Engineer of BHU, and Jwala Prasad (1872–1944), member of the Indian Engineering Services (IES).[64] The first buildings to be completed there were those of the Faculty of Arts and departments of Physics and Chemistry. These incorporated elements of temple architecture such as '*pidhas* (pyramidal roofs) and *sikharas* (spires)'. Further, their entrances comprised 'pillared porches, characteristic of temples'. These buildings were also graced with '*chhatris* (small, pillared pavilions topped by domes)' and '*chhajja[s]* (balconies)' (like traditional palaces and forts of Hindu rulers). But for the pillared porches, the hostels at the Nagwa campus were bestowed with these architectural elements too.[65] BHU, thus, self-consciously projected a Hindu image through the construction of its academic and residential blocks.

Appearance apart, the architecture of the Nagwa campus also gave the institution a very obviously Hindu ambience. As we infer from the observations of Leah Renold, the apparel and demeanour of professors and students (again, self-consciously Hindu) as well as the simple vegetarian fare served in the hostels contributed to this ambience.[66] It was almost as though BHU was a modern day *gurukul*, or forest hermitage, attracting seekers of knowledge. For instance, the professors at BHU 'were addressed by students as guru*ji* and ... accorded similar gestures of respect as traditional gurus and elders; when students appeared before their professors, they knelt and touched ... [their] feet'. This was regardless of whether they were Brahmin or non-Brahmin.[67] Scholars at BHU punctiliously adhered to the Hindu ethos of the giver of knowledge being worthy of reverence, their social background or identity notwithstanding.

The professors on their part were distinguished by their kind-heartedness towards students. They, as we learn, were remarkably accessible and even went to the extent of hosting them in their homes. The BHU faculty, perhaps, deliberately behaved to contrast the aloofness of the western professors in the other universities of British-ruled India.[68] Teacher-student relations at BHU, thus, were exceptionally warm and close in a manner very redolent of the indigenous educational heritage of India.

BHU, as we know, meant to provide mandatory religious instruction to all its Hindu students. This necessitated a textbook of Hinduism. Malaviya had commissioned a certain Pandit Umapati Dvivedi to write one already in 1906, when a Hindu university seemed but a dim future prospect. Dvivedi came up with a four volume Sanskrit-Hindi text in 1912. Titled *Sanatanadharmoddhara*, it was like 'a Purana in its diverse range of content and style'.[69] The work was too unwieldy and hard to read to serve as a textbook. Consequently, once BHU became operational, Malaviya rejected it in favour of *Sanātana Dharma: An Advanced Text-Book of Hindu Religion and Ethics*. It had originally been drafted by Besant in 1901[70] for religious instruction at the Central Hindu College with material supplied by Dr Bhagvan Das (1869–1958),[71] the institution's secretary. She organized the eleven chapters of this primer under three rubrics, namely, 'Basic Hindu Religious Ideas', 'General Hindu Religious Customs and Rites', and 'Ethical Teachings'.[72] The textbook, in this way, provided a very reasonable overview of Hindu spiritual beliefs, orthopraxis, and mores along with their scriptural underpinnings. Significantly, it did so with brevity and in an accessible language. *Sanātana Dharma*, thus, was concise and represented its subject with 'clarity and simplicity'. The textbook focused on the commonalities that united Hindus irrespective of sectarian differences. Resultantly, it portrayed Hinduism 'in a … graspable form … amenable to classroom instruction'.[73] Nevertheless, despite being competently authored, as we discover, it failed to enthuse its targeted audience.

Scholars at BHU, it seems, were not quite keen on receiving religious instruction. The lectures on Hindu religion, as a result, were not very well attended. Things came to such a pass that BHU even considered punishing students for skipping them. Malaviya, however, ensured that this was not done, since in his view it was 'un-Hindu to force anyone to be religious'. Religious instruction continued to be nominally compulsory for all students professing the Hindu faith. But their attendance in the religion classes was not closely monitored. Nor was the religion exam made too taxing. It was kept at a level that students would not find it too difficult to pass. BHU, as a result, according to Leah Renold, failed to foster among students the synthetic sense of Hindu religion provided in *Sanātana Dharma*.[74]

As the attempt at inculcating religiosity through formal instruction was not very successful, the university sought to make the overall ambience of the campus religious instead. Students, writes Leah Renold, were encouraged to pray every morning and evening[75] and attend sermons on the Bhagavad Gita on Sundays.[76] Compulsion was avoided in both regards. BHU preferred that students prayed and listened to the sermons voluntarily. The latter, thus, were poorly attended like the religion classes. Attendance at the Bhagavad Gita sermons would be good only if they were given by Radhakrishnan himself.[77] Malaviya's successor to BHU's Vice-Chancellorship was a world-renowned philosopher.

While being unpopular with students, there were times when compulsory religious instruction was at the centre of controversies in the university Court. For instance, when BHU commenced tuitions in 1917, some of its members were apprehensive about the difficulty of defining 'Hindu' and 'Hinduism' and giving 'such religious instruction' that is acceptable to all Hindus.[78] It was pointed out to them that definitional concerns had not come in the way when the Central Hindu College conducted classes in the Hindu religion. They were also assured that BHU would teach Hinduism in terms of the 'tenets and principles' shared by its 'principal denominations'.[79]

Parleys broke out in the Court over the religion classes once again in 1919. This was due to a resolution passed by the Faculty of Theology (responsible for conducting them) on 7 March. It demanded that 'only Brahmins following strictly the ancient traditional rules of sadachar (morality) should be appointed as religious instructors and lecturers in the Benares Hindu University'.[80] The resolution, it seems, put Malaviya in something like a quandary. He wanted the cooperation of Hindu society at large to build up BHU.[81] Thus, alienating any segments or groups of Hindus was not an option for him. However, being deeply orthodox, Malaviya also sympathized with the position taken by the Faculty of Theology (as did others like him at BHU, cases in point being Mahamahopadhyaya Pandit Lakshmana Dravid Shastri and Pandit Prabhu Datt Shastri).[82] He took it upon himself to explain it to the Court at its annual meeting on 11 December 1920. Malaviya argued that it was the 'general sentiment' among Hindus:

> [T]he persons to be appointed as religious instructors at … [BHU] should not only be endowed with learning and piety … they should also be of the class whose special duty it was according to the ancient religious traditions of the country to impart religious training.[83]

In effect, thus, he took the view that the Faculty of Theology had only articulated what was a general consensus within Hindu society through its resolution. He assured the Court that the 'recommendation of the Faculty was not made out of any prejudice against non-Brahmin scholars, but simply with a view to act in conformity with the old traditions'.[84]

The controversy, however, dragged on and was resolved only when a compromise resolution was adopted at the next annual meeting of the Court on 14 December 1921. Moved by the apparently reform-minded Babu Jnanendranath Basu, it went as follows:

> That the Faculty of Theology should appoint Lecturers in Hindu Religion in accordance with a liberal interpretation, in a catholic spirit, of the Manava Dharma Shastra, without laying down any policy which may injure the feelings of any section of the [Hindu] community.[85]

In other words, as we understand, the Court urged the Faculty of Theology to abjure excessive rigidity and consider the possibility of appointing non-Brahmins to teach the religion classes within the framework of the Manusmriti. The practicability of this position apart, both orthodox and reformists at BHU were for the present satisfied. In theory at least the College of Theology could now consider hiring non-Brahmin teachers. In terms of student intake, however, it continued to restrict itself to Brahmins as before. This was due to a clause in the regulations of BHU 'that said that… [the] courses related to the Vedas would be open to only those candidates who, according to the accepted Hindu usage, … [are] qualified to officiate at Hindu religious ceremonials and rituals.'[86] Simply put, the university's position was that a person must be authorized by tradition to oversee the sacred rites to receive instruction in the Vedas. Hence, being a Brahmin was an imperative to enrol at the College of Theology. Being male was an imperative too. BHU would refuse admission to a woman scholar in the College of Theology in 1945 (despite being, it seems, a Brahmin).[87] Presumably, this was because orthodox Hindu usage does not countenance female priests.

BHU was lenient when students were indifferent towards religious instruction. However, it was rather strict in ensuring that their conduct is in conformity with Hindu moral values. Smoking and consumption of alcohol, thus, were forbidden on the campus. Neither were paan (betel leaf) shops allowed there. The university, in this way, kept students from what it thought were vices from the point of view of Hindu morality as a part of the education it imparted. Also, BHU students were forbidden from hunting and fishing and had to abjure meat while on campus. The food served in the hostels was strictly vegetarian and comprised rice, lentils, and vegetables. The few European professors in the employ of the university (for instance, the English principal of the College of Engineering, Charles King) boarded and dined at a 'non-vegetarian hostel' at the far end of the campus.

Interestingly, however, as it enforced its conception of Hindu dietary norms, the university did not bother with the rules of commensality then prevailing within Hindu society. Students of all jati groups dined together in BHU hostels.[88] In fact, there was no status-based segregation of students at BHU in any form. They lived in the same hostels regardless of their social backgrounds or identities. This is significant because this was not yet the norm in Indian educational institutions. For example, hostels were allotted as per caste at the Agra College.[89] BHU did, however, segregate the genders to an extent. Women students, thus, 'were not offered all the courses of study open to men'. The Women's College at BHU was off-limits to the male students. If one of them wanted to deliver a message to a woman scholar enrolled there, it had to be done through the college warden or superintendent.

The mobility of women students was restricted too. They were permitted by the warden to leave the college premises only in groups, strictly to visit a temple or for shopping. Both male and female students had to be back at their hostels for roll call by 7 p.m. in winter and 8 p.m. in summer.[90] There was no dress code as such at BHU. However, most students preferred to wear dhotis, kurtas, and saris.[91] Sartorially, they chose to look Hindu. The exception was the College of Engineering where students dressed in formal Western attire.[92]

Along with morality, as we gather, BHU sought to inculcate in students a full and proper sense of what it meant to be Hindu in terms of cultural and religious praxis. We have already seen how the university motivated them to pray and listen to expositions of the Bhagavad Gita. Alongside, BHU enthusiastically observed the major Hindu holidays such as Holi, Shiva Ratri, and Dussehra. This was an essential feature of campus life involving, as Leah Renold puts it, 'much festivity'. For instance, this is how the university celebrated Basant Panchami in 1923:

> Several hundred students of the Nagwa hostels met on 22 January in the Oriental College.... The hall was decorated and a lively and instructive *katha* was given by Pandit Vinayak Rao of Brahmaghat accompanied by fine music which was relished by all. Professor Chinnaswami spoke in Sanskrit and several students said classical Sanskrit *slokas* descriptive of spring. It was a real feast for the eyes to see groups of young men dressed in yellow and pink, the whole scene being the inauguration of *Basant*. The VC conducted the Saraswati Puja.[93]

The foregoing description appeared in the *Central Hindu College Magazine* (it was renamed *BHU Magazine* in 1925). Students, as it shows, participated actively and in a big way in the observance of Basant Panchami at BHU. The enthusiastic involvement of students seems to have been the norm during every festival celebrated by the university. Scholars at BHU, in this way, appear to have periodically partaken in Hindu 'communitas', or liminal situations demonstrating the oneness of all Hindus, particularistic differences of jati or place of origin notwithstanding.[94] In other words, as we imagine, the religious festivals at BHU drew them all together and gave them the tangible experience of an essential and shared Hinduness. BHU, thus, replicated or expressed the effort at greater cohesion that generally characterized Hindu society at this historical juncture.

BHU students acquired the important Hindu value of seva, or service, through participation in certain campus initiatives. For example, the Seva Samiti was established at the university in 1921. It was an organization dedicated to social service. As we observe, the Seva Samiti fostered considerable student activism. Its cadre would go out into villages to spread awareness regarding healthcare, sanitation, and khadi. They would also help flood victims. The Seva Samiti ran with money donated by students. It did considerable good work and drew praise from none other than the Vice-Chancellor of Aligarh Muslim University (AMU), Aftab Alam Khan. Addressing the All-India Mohammadan Educational Conference in 1924, he termed the student activists of the Seva Samiti 'Hindu missionaries' and held them up as examples for Muslim youth. He, informs Leah Renold, 'called upon the Muslims to educate their students to be as sacrificial as … [these] Hindu students.'[95]

BHU sought to make physical education a part of academics and undertook to provide the requisite facilities to students. The university began construction of a gymnasium in 1929 with funds expressly raised for the purpose.[96] Further, Malaviya was keen on scholars receiving military training. It is possible that he thought that they would grow in confidence and acquire well-rounded personalities because of it. He, consequently, desired to raise a University Training Corps. Malaviya was permitted to form two platoons thereof by Viceroy Lord Reading (1860–1935) when he came to BHU in 1921. Later, in 1927, his successor Lord Irwin (1881–1959) sanctioned another platoon of BHU's Training Corps during a visit to the university. This was since the initiative was tremendously popular with (male) students and large numbers of them desired to join it (it does not appear to have been open to women scholars). Seemingly well drilled and disciplined, BHU's Training Corps were very successful and frequently triumphed over their counterparts from other universities in competitions. They won the Efficiency Cup, apparently some annual contest of various university training corps, every year from 1925 to 1928 and again in 1929 and 1930.[97] In 1945, BHU introduced a scheme of compulsory physical education for all its students as an experiment. It required scholars 'to go through a systematic course of physical drill for a period of two years at least'.[98]

BHU, as we have seen, underwent considerable financial struggles and its expansion plans might even have been briefly thwarted by lack of funds. Nevertheless, the university's growth in terms of colleges, departments, and academic programmes in the pre-independent period was still quite significant. It established a Teacher's

Training College[99] and began a Department of Mechanical Engineering in 1918.[100] BHU's Department of Geology became operational in 1922.[101] The university established a College of Law next year,[102] while its College of Ayurveda began conducting classes in the 1924–25 academic session.[103] The Faculty of Medicine and Surgery (Ayurveda) came into existence at BHU in 1928,[104] as did the College for Women.[105] It began the construction of an Institute of Agricultural Research in 1929 with a grant of Rs 3 lakh from Maharaja Sir Umaid Singh of Jodhpur (1903–47).[106] The institute would be raised to the status of a full-fledged college in 1944.[107] Diploma courses in soap manufacture, metal enamelling, and pottery and porcelain were started at BHU in 1932. Earlier, in 1930, it had instituted a diploma in ceramics technology. BSc (Industrial Chemistry) and MSc (Industrial Chemistry) had their inception at the university in 1935.[108] In 1936, BHU established the Faculty of Technology and put under its purview engineering, mining and metallurgy, industrial chemistry, pharmaceutical chemistry, and agriculture.[109] The university established the Sanskrit Mahavidyalaya by amalgamating the Colleges of Oriental Learning and Theology in 1946[110] (Malaviya's attempt of absorbing the Government Sanskrit College had earlier ended in failure). All through, it tried to discharge its mission of preserving Indic traditions and frameworks of knowledge with sincerity. This was not just in terms of what was taught at the Colleges of Oriental Learning and Theology. BHU also sought to adopt Indian languages as mediums of instruction and tried to develop textbooks in them.[111] In 1947, when the country attained independence from British rule, it seriously considered conducting classes in Hindi alone.[112]

Politics at BHU

As we saw, Gandhi rather crudely used BHU's foundation stone-laying ceremony to advance his own politics and, perhaps, improve his prospects as a national-level leader (when he was not yet one). The institution, in this way, had a political beginning despite itself. The populist, agitational politics Gandhi was in the process of formulating headlong clashed with the 'moderate' political approach (vocally represented by Besant) on the occasion. In due course, BHU became a site of politics in its own way, as is natural in any enterprise involving many human actors. Those involved in running the institution sometimes had mutually opposed or conflicting points of view and adopted stratagems to prevail over their adversaries.

We have already observed how the premature and sudden step down of Sivaswamy Aiyar from the university's Vice-Chancellorship might have been because of a lack of genuine consensus in the Court regarding his appointment. The dissenting party, thus, refused him their cooperation and eventually got rid of him. Again, internal politics at BHU could be occasioned by the clash of orthodox and reformist positions, as it happened around the question of faculty appointments at the College of Theology.

Moreover, BHU students, being keen and intelligent youth, contributed to the overall political ambience of the institution with their intellectual dabbling. They, for instance, critically examined the validity of nationalism as a sentiment and looked at Indian politics from the point of view of Hindu–Muslim relations in the pages of *BHU Magazine*.[113] Regardless of the fact that life on campus was overwritten by Hindu spiritual and moral values, some BHU students even went to the extent of systematically studying

Marxism, an atheist and radically anti-tradition framework of thought. Personally, Malaviya was averse to the Marxist worldview. Nevertheless, he kept from interfering, being a believer in freedom of speech.[114] Thus, as we imagine, numbers of BHU students freely voiced positions derived from Marxist tenets. The university parliament, established to train students in self-government, the hostel unions, and various students' associations gave rise to their own share of politics.[115]

A deeply patriotic lot, students and teachers at BHU naturally responded to the trends and initiatives in the ongoing struggle for national independence. The Non-Cooperation Movement, as a result, became an intensely political episode for the fledgling institution and left it fractured. Chiefly, this was because Gandhi yet again made BHU a pretext to advance his agenda and point of view.

From the programmatic standpoint, one of the key features of the Non-Cooperation Movement was the boycott of government-run and government-funded educational institutions. Gandhi's idea was to replace them with nationalist schools, colleges, and universities. Thus, institutions like the Gujrat Vidyapith, Behar [sic.] Vidyapith, Kashi Vidyapith, Bengal National University, Tilak Maharashtra Vidyapeeth, Jamia Millia Islamia, etc., were established during the Non-Cooperation Movement.[116] They were all inspired by the Gandhian vision for a framework of national education.

BHU became the focus of Gandhi's disapproval because it had been established under an act of the colonial regime and received an annual endowment from it. He made an open bid to subvert the institution as he visited its campus on 27 November 1920. Addressing the students (with Malaviya in attendance), Gandhi said that a Hindu education is impossible in a 'government-sponsored university'. He demanded that BHU refuse government grants and forfeit its charter (the provisions of BHU Act). Gandhi also urged the students to discontinue their studies.[117] In effect, he sought to destroy BHU altogether.

Displaying remarkable nobility of spirit, Malaviya made no harsh or angry retort to Gandhi. In his response, he merely pointed out what he thought were the problems in the Non-Cooperation programme and asked the students to arrive at a decision only after a careful consideration of the issues.[118] Malaviya, did not see sense in an eschewal of colonial education without a concomitant boycott of the railways, postal and telegraph services, and municipalities (that is, the civic amenities provided by the regime). The fact that the Montagu-Chelmsford Reforms of 1919 had made education a 'transferred' subject (the purview of an elected Indian representative) also contributed to his scepticism.

As for BHU, Malaviya's position was that it enjoyed autonomy, and that the government did not interfere in its functioning. On the other hand, the financial assistance it received from the government was but Indian money (since it came from the taxes paid by Indians).[119] Thus, Malaviya thought that BHU was not doing anything wrong in accepting endowments from the regime. His compelling logic notwithstanding, about 200 students left BHU in the wake of Gandhi's visit. Some teachers and staff members quit too. Among the former was the brilliant Acharya J.B. Kriplani (1888–1982).[120] He would later join Kashi Vidyapith, an initiative personally backed by Gandhi.

As far as possible, Malaviya's policy was to shield BHU from all-India politics (and the periodic agitations it generated), even if it meant going against the grain of nationalist opinion. He, thus, hosted the Prince of Wales, Edward VIII (1894–1972), on campus and conferred upon him an honorary degree of Doctor of Letters in 1921.[121] This was right in the middle of the Non-Cooperation Movement and in defiance of the Congress's call to boycott the Prince's visit to India. Malaviya, it seems, risked widespread opprobrium because he did not want BHU to go back on an invitation it had extended to the British heir apparent much previously. Being a thorough gentleman, he is liable to have found this an extremely unseemly thing to do so.

One must not think that Malaviya sought to politically sequester the campus to ingratiate himself and BHU with colonial authorities. His wish was that the chief focus of students is on education. Yet, if they chose to involve themselves in nationalist agitation, he would not bar their way. For instance, when the Civil Disobedience Movement began in 1930, he advised them to prioritize their own intellectual, moral, and physical education before going forth to serve the nation. Nevertheless, he did not hinder the students who had made up their minds to participate.[122] Neither did the university comply when the government demanded that action be taken against them.[123]

Malaviya's advise to BHU students at the time of the Quit India agitation was not to resort to any action that is against the teachings of Gandhi.[124] Once again, he did not prevent them from joining in. As it turned out, BHU students did so in such great numbers that the colonial police and military stormed and evacuated the campus on 19 August.[125] BHU was a nationalist bastion. There were no king and empire loyalists there.

5

BHU after Independence: Assault upon Identity (1948–65)

A Few Mixed Years

Radhakrishnan was in his third term as BHU's Vice-Chancellor when India attained independence from British rule. He was, by this time, quite reluctant to continue in this position. As a matter of fact, he wished to return full-time to the University of Oxford, where he was the Spalding Professor of Eastern Religion and Ethics,[1] back in 1945, after completing his second stint of Vice-Chancellorship. However, Radhakrishnan changed his mind when Malaviya persuaded him not to sever ties with BHU. In deference to his wish, he consented to be re-appointed Vice-Chancellor by the Court for three more years. The Court, for its part, framed a special statute to help him attend to his duties at Oxford. It allowed Radhakrishnan to depute one of its members to the Vice-Chancellor's responsibilities if he had to leave India for more than three months.[2] Apparently, as far as Radhakrishnan was concerned, this did not help matters much. The chief mode of travel between continents was still the passenger ship and it took about three weeks to sail from India to Great Britain. In view of this situation,

Radhakrishnan is unlikely to have found it very feasible or practical to divide time between Oxford and Banaras.

Eventually, in March 1947, Radhakrishnan urged the university to expeditiously find his replacement. He was, as he put it, finding it 'impossible' to continue as the Vice-Chancellor.[3] A few months later, in October, he left for Oxford.[4] Finally, Radhakrishnan sent in his resignation in December.[5]

Radhakrishnan's successor to the Vice-Chancellorship of BHU was Dr Amarnath Jha (1897–1955). He was appointed to the position by the Court on 11 January 1948. The Court also passed a resolution on this occasion, moved by Dr Hriday Nath Kunzru (1887–1978), expressing its 'grateful appreciation of the services rendered by … [Radhakrishnan] to the University during the past eight years'.[6] It recalled how he had placed the institution on a 'secure financial foundation' displayed 'profound grasp' of its problems, and spread its fame 'wherever he had gone'.[7]

Dr Jha, however, held his office only until the end of 1948. This was because his appointment was something of a stop-gap arrangement, being for the remainder of Radhakrishnan's term. The Court met again to find his replacement on 5 December 1948. After some deliberation, it decided on Pandit Govind Malaviya (1902–61).[8] A politician and educationist, he was the youngest son of Madan Mohan Malaviya and an alumnus of BHU.

Govind Malaviya's stint as the Vice-Chancellor turned out to be rather brief too. He abruptly resigned in April 1951 when he came to think that the Court lacks confidence in his academic and administrative competence.[9]

A considerable drama took place in the wake of Govind Malaviya's impulsive act. The Court first accepted his resignation and then sought to re-elect him the Vice-Chancellor for a period of three-years.[10] Eventually, after exchanging letters with the Court for five months, the President of India, Dr Rajendra Parsad (1884–1963), adjudged Govind Malaviya's re-election to the Vice-Chancellorship untenable in his capacity as the Visitor to BHU.[11] He followed up by appointing Acharya Narendra Deva (1889–1956), a distinguished educationist and much respected political leader, as BHU's Vice-Chancellor for a period of six years.[12] Deva assumed office in December 1951.

Unfortunately, Deva's health failed to keep up with his responsibilities and he resigned at the end of 1953, after completing a mere two years of his term. Deva was persuaded to stay on for the time being, while his letter of resignation was forwarded to the Visitor. His health, however, continued to deteriorate. At long last, in May 1954, Deva wrote to the Visitor requesting to be relieved of his duties. In slightly more than six years, a third Vice-Chancellor had vacated office at BHU.

Deva's successor was Dr C.P. Ramaswami Aiyar (1879–1966). His name was proposed by BHU's (newfangled) Executive Council and approved by the Visitor in July 1954. Like Deva, Aiyar was appointed Vice-Chancellor for six years.[13]

Aiyar brought both enthusiasm and efficiency to his role. He sought to make BHU a purveyor of enlightenment in the form of a steady stream of books on science, art, literature, drama, and poetry. Aiyar also set about providing adequate residences and financial stability to the faculty and sufficient amenities for a conducive academic environment for students. All along, he maintained a gentle but firm discipline.[14] Aiyar, in other words, started off as the Vice-Chancellor of BHU on an extremely promising note. However, he too ended up stepping down prematurely. Aiyar submitted his resignation in March 1956. Apparently, this was on grounds of health and in view of some commitments he had.[15]

Aiyar's successor was Dr V.S. Jha.[16] Again, he resigned before his full tenure of six years was up. Jha quit in December 1959,[17] after completing somewhat more than half of it. It now fell upon N.H. Bhagwati (1894–1970) to provide BHU the stability of leadership it desperately needed. Appointed the Vice-Chancellor in April 1960,[18] he discharged his office for the full six years. This was, as we shall see, despite BHU erupting in complete turmoil at one point. Bhagwati, in this way, was an astute administrator and capable of handling a difficult situation.

BHU continued to grow academically amid the rapid coming and going of Vice-Chancellors. The university started a College of Indology and absorbed Bharat Kala Bhavan in 1950. Established in 1920 as Bharat Kala Parishad, the latter was an institution dedicated to the promotion and preservation of Indian art and culture. Its rich collection of paintings, sculptures, textiles, and ancient coins was transferred to BHU.[19] The university, resultantly, found itself in possession of a veritable treasure trove of heritage with immense educational value.

The College of Ayurveda at BHU was renamed the College of Medical Sciences and an MBBS course was begun there in September 1960. This was the most significant addition to the institution's repertoire of courses since independence. The College of Medical Sciences was inaugurated by Dr D.P. Karmakar (1902–91), Minister of State for Health, on 24 December 1960. In keeping with BHU's objective of preserving and imparting Indian knowledge, the MBBS course included the basics of Ayurveda and was not entirely based on Western medicine.[20]

In 1965, the endpoint of this narrative and a cataclysmic year in which the institution faced a major assault upon its identity, BHU comprised thirteen full-fledged colleges. Besides the Colleges of Medical Sciences and Indology, these were the Samskrit Mahavidyalaya, Central Hindu College, Teachers' Training College, College of Science, Women's College, Law College, College of Music and Fine Arts, Engineering College, College of Technology, College of Agriculture, and the College of Mining and Metallurgy. Further, the university ran a Post-Graduate Institute of Indian Medicine. Approximately 8,300 students studied there while it employed about 900 faculty.[21]

A major episode at BHU after independence was the observance of Malaviya's birth centenary. In preparation, the university renovated the Malaviya Bhawan, where Malaviya had lived and breathed his last, on campus. It also installed his white marble bust on the building's premises. Inaugurated on 25 December 1961 by Radhakrishnan, now the Vice President of India, the birth centenary celebrations lasted a year and comprised a whole series of small and big events. These had been planned by an all-India committee chaired by none other than the Prime Minister, Jawaharlal Nehru. An enormous throng of about one lakh attended the inauguration. The Vice-Chancellor of the university as well as the Vice President gave heartfelt tributes to Malaviya on the occasion. BHU also urged its alumni across the country to organize their own celebrations to observe Malaviya's birth centenary.[22]

As in the years before independence, BHU was committed to the all-round development of its students. In 1962, when the country faced Chinese aggression, the university introduced compulsory military training for them. The idea, it seems was to inculcate in students the capacity, lest the need arose, to rally in defence of the nation. Consequently, they would undergo the soldiers' drill twice a week.[23]

BHU was also keen on ensuring that students remain in touch with the Hindu spiritual values. Considering its denominational identity as an institution, this was but natural. Malaviya had always wanted a temple on campus. Unfortunately, he passed away without fulfilling this wish. The construction of a Shiva temple eventually began at BHU in 1948. Work proceeded slowly, apparently due to the paucity of funds, and it was consecrated on Shiva Ratri in 1958. The shrine, however, was not structurally complete yet. It took until 1965 to finish raising its spire.[24]

Alongside spiritual values, BHU inculcated in its students the requisite skills and awareness to participate in civil society and public life. To this end, a mock students' parliament had been established at the institution before independence. The University Union came into existence at BHU as a participatory students' body in 1948. Meant to function under the guidance of the Speaker of the parliament, a faculty member, its objectives were as follows:

1) To promote patriotism, public spirit, education in citizenship and the growth of a disciplined life among the students of the University;
2) To promote the academic, social and cultural welfare of the students of the University;
3) To promote the growth of a sense of responsibility among the students and thus to afford them opportunities to participate in public life.[25]

The students' parliament endured and was brought to overlap with the University Union in some ways. The President of the Union was now the Premier of the parliament and was to be elected in accordance with its constitution. Also, the parliament elected the General Secretary of the Union while its Privy Council served as its General Council.[26]

The University Union was replaced by BHU Students' Association in 1962. It sought to consolidate all students' initiatives at the university and was meant to pursue the following objectives:

1) To foster fellow-feeling and disciplined corporate life among the students of the University;
2) To promote the intellectual and cultural advancement of the students of the University;
3) To promote the study and discussion of subjects of national and international importance;
4) To uphold and foster the development of the moral and spiritual values of the student community;
5) To promote the growth of a sense of civic responsibility among the students of the University and, thereby, to prepare them for shouldering the civic responsibilities of the democratic state;
6) To promote among the students of the University the sense of national unity; and
7) Any other object which, in the opinion of the Standing Committee of the Academic Council, is conducive to the welfare and advancement of the student community.

Except for students in the Pre-University Course, the Association comprised all students at BHU. All the university faculty and administrative staff were its members too.[27]

The students' parliament became a 'division' within the Association. It also included a cultural centre as a second division. Among the latter's tasks were organizing cultural programmes, programmes relevant to the promotion of national unity and 'moral, spiritual, cultural and social welfare' and social gatherings. The Association carried out its activities in close collaboration with the Dean of Students.[28]

As in the pre-independent years, politics was a part of campus life. We have already seen how BHU students actively participated in the Gandhian mass mobilizations against the colonial regime. The campus, in this way, showed a proclivity for agitation. Along with the political awareness among students, as we find, this was also due to unionization among the university's workers. Organized as the Mazdoor Sangh, the Class IV staff of BHU—peons, 'servants', laboratory bearers, et. al—went on strike on 21 April 1948 demanding a revision of their pay scales. The university authorities refused to comply and dismissed the striking workers while arranging for temporary substitutes to take their place. Eventually, the strike petered out and by the end of May many Class IV employees applied for re-employment and returned to work.[29]

The campus was restive again a decade later when a largescale students' agitation broke out in July 1958. It sought the removal of the Acting Principal of the Ayurvedic College. By September, it had snowballed to the extent that the residences of the Pro-Vice-Chancellor and Registrar as well as the Central Office were picketed. As the agitation showed signs of turning violent, the Executive Council decided to close the university. The announcement was made on 7 October and all students residing on campus were ordered to leave for their homes. The university reopened in a phased manner 13 November onwards, after more than a month.[30]

The Banaras Hindu University (Amendment) Bill

The attempt on the part of the government to dilute or efface BHU's denominational identity began immediately after independence. It first contemplated amending the BHU Act (passed in 1915) and remove 'Hindu' from the institution's name in 1948. As the University Court learnt about this, it expressed its strong disapproval through a resolution.[31]

Again, in 1949, the report of the University Education Commission recommended that 'the denominational character of the University Court be eliminated'.[32] In other words, it urged the government to allow non-Hindus to serve on BHU's chief administrative body. It did so about a couple of years later through the Benares Hindu University (Amendment) Act, 1951.[33] After receiving Presidential assent on 20 October, it came into force on 3 November.[34]

Then, in 1958, the government of India acted on the recommendations of the Banaras Hindu University Enquiry Committee (headed by Dr A.L. Mudaliar, 1887–1974) and promulgated the Banaras Hindu University (Amendment) Ordinance. It significantly reduced the university's autonomy by curtailing the powers of the Court. From being the paramount administrative body of BHU, it was reduced to an advisory position vis-à-vis the Visitor, or the President of India. The President was also given the power to appoint twenty-nine people of his choice to the Court.[35]

As we see it, the government now arrogated to itself the power of interfering in BHU's administrative matters through the President. More importantly, it could, if it wished, use the President to include a significant number of non-Hindus in the Court and dilute BHU's denominational identity in an underhand way. Nevertheless, it chose to launch a direct assault upon it a few years later.

Rajya Sabha, the upper house of the Indian parliament, began discussing the Banaras Hindu University (Amendment) Bill, 1964 on 10 November 1965. It sought to rename BHU as 'Madan Mohan Malaviya Kashi Vishwavidyalaya'. The idea, the Minister of Education, M.C. Chagla (1900–81),[36] told the house, was to 'perpetuate the memory of late Pandit Madan Mohan Malaviya'.[37] Also, the incumbent Congress government thought that the denominational character of BHU was not in keeping with its status as per the constitution. Hence, it wished to erase 'Hindu' from its name.

As Chagla said in the Rajya Sabha on 16 November after it passed the bill:

> [T]he Banaras Hindu University is a national University. It is a national University under the Constitution and in changing the name what we have done is to give a name that ... [is] in substance correct under the Constitution. The word 'Hindu' was opposed to the constitutional aspect of this institution ... no disrespect whatsoever is meant to Hinduism or to the expression 'Hindu' ... today when we have adopted a secular philosophy ... it is necessary to remove any doubt or suspicion about our secularism. Although we have removed the 'Hindu' we have got the name Madan Mohan Malaviya and the word 'Kashi' both of which represent the highest, the best and the noblest in Hindu culture, Hindu philosophy and Hindu history... this brings out even more emphatically the philosophy and culture for which the Banaras University stands.[38]

Chagla, thus, took the view that it was necessary to align BHU with the secularism enshrined in the constitution and emphasize its national character. This could be done only by giving it a name that did not sound particularistic from the cultural or religious point of view. Chagla did not want BHU to make an obvious declaration of its denominational nature. As far as he was concerned, 'Madan Mohan Malaviya' and 'Kashi' sufficed to indicate all that was Hindu about the institution.

The Congressmen who participated in the discussion on the bill zealously seconded the Minister of Education. For instance, G.S. Pathak (1896–1982), a member of the upper house from UP,[39] declaimed the following on 10 November:

> It [BHU] is an institution of national importance. It belongs to the entire nation … Pandit Madan Mohan Malaviya was the founder of this University and he followed some ideals. Those ideals are reflected in some of the features of this University and it would be very desirable that the name of Madan Mohan Malaviya be associated with this University and the name 'Hindu' be dropped.[40]

Pathak somehow missed it altogether that Malaviya's ideals derived from a deep attachment to Hindu religious beliefs and that he had wished BHU to represent and regenerate Hindu society.

N. Narotham Reddy (1921–84) was a Rajya Sabha member from Andhra Pradesh.[41] Addressing the house after Pathak, he pleaded that 'the word "Hindu" should not be there' [in 'Banaras Hindu University']. He preferred a name for the institution that excluded it, even if it meant renaming it (rather baldly) as 'Banaras University.'[42]

The gentleman was definitely very averse to the denominational character of BHU and a passionate advocate of secularism as interpreted by his party.

Reddy was followed by Pandit Sham Sundar Narain Tankha (1898–1985). Like Pathak, he also represented UP in the upper house.[43] Pandit Tankha agreed with Reddy and made the following observation:

> We are a secular state according to the constitution... Then why should we have any appellation in the name of the [Banaras Hindu] university which connotes a particular religion in it... Therefore, for a secular state it would be wrong thing to say that the University should be called 'Banaras Hindu University'. 'Banaras University' is quite good.[44]

He, in other words, seemed to take the same view of secularism as Reddy and wished to rid BHU of its denominational identity. Pandit Tankha, however, was not very keen that the university be renamed after Malaviya, lest it fail to do justice to his greatness. Instead, he recommended that it is given a name which, as he alleged, was originally chosen by Malaviya. Pandit Tankha, apparently, wanted BHU to project a purely spatial identity without evoking any denominational or communitarian ties. If not 'Banaras University', thus, he wanted the institution to be called 'Kashi Vishwa-Vidyalay':

> [If] ... the name should be after that great man Madan Mohan Malaviya, who founded the University, I would have no objection.... But what I am afraid of is that if you give a great man's name to an institution and if that institution at a later date may fall into evil days, and cannot keep up to the traditions of its founder or of that great man,

> then, I am afraid, it will bring a bad name on that great man himself. Therefore to associate any institution, a teaching institution particularly, with a great man's name would not be a right thing to do.... But I think the name which Pandit Madan Mohan Malaviya himself suggested namely 'The Kashi Vishwa-Vidyalay' is quite appropriate. If any change has to be made after dropping the word 'Hindu' and if it is to be named as 'the Kashi Vishwa-Vidyalay', that too is acceptable to me ... if the hon. [Education] Minister desires it to be named after the great Pandit Madan Mohan Malaviya, well, the House will be only too glad to name it after him. But as I have said, what I am afraid of is as to whether it would live up to his great ideals.[45]

It seems Tankha was deliberately misleading the house to serve the cause of secularism. Or he was altogether ignorant of BHU's history. As we have seen in the previous chapters, the names used by Malaviya in the two prospectuses he authored for the institution were respectively 'Hindu University' and the 'Hindu University of Benares'. At no point, as far as we know, did he suggest or use the name 'Kashi Vishwa-Vidyalay'.

Dr Tara Chand (1888–1973), historian and former Vice-Chancellor of Allahabad University, joined the discussion on 11 November. A nominated member of the upper house,[46] his choice was the same as Pandit Tankha's. However, Dr Chand suggested that BHU be renamed after Kashi because of the pilgrimage's great civilizational vintage:

> [W]e may call ... [BHU] Kashi Vishwavidyalaya, ... Kashi is undoubtedly a name which is as old as India. It occurs in the Atharva Veda. It occurs in all the sacred literature of the Hindus, in the Buddhist literature also and in the various

> other books which we hold sacred in India. Therefore, the term 'Kashi' possibly, probably in fact, brings to our mind the history of an entire culture over 4,000 and 5,000 years and therefore, undoubtedly it would be a good thing if this university is named Kashi Vishwavidyalaya.

At the same time, unlike Tankha, he was not averse to the idea of BHU bearing Malaviya's name if it came to that. Dr Tara Chand thought that Malaviya fully deserved to be commemorated in this way. As he put it:

> [N]ow that he [Malaviya] has passed away … it would be very graceful on our part to do so [rename BHU after him] it would be recognizing the services of one of the greatest men that India produced in the 19th century, of one who has done in a long life a great deal more than many men have done for the uplift of the country – should not this grateful generation recognize and associate his name with the University?[47]

The politically unaffiliated A.D. Mani (1910–78) supported renaming BHU to demonstrate India's secular credentials to Pakistan, although he felt that the new name was something of a mouthful. A member of the Rajya Sabha from Madhya Pradesh (MP),[48] he spoke on the bill on 15 November:

> It will be conceded by all that the Indian culture is an amalgam of various cultures and Hindu culture perhaps forms the dominant trend in that amalgam but we have to take into account the strident propaganda which has been done by Pakistan against India and by its accusations that the Indian society is a Hindu form of society. If we believe in a secular form of society, there is no way but to accept

> the amendment moved by the Minister, namely, that the title should be changed and it should be called the Madan Mohan Malaviya Kashi Vishwavidyalaya ... [I] know that it is a cumbrous name. It is not easy to roll one's tongue [around it] as in the case of the Banaras Hindu University but for the sake of maintaining our secular form of society, I would suggest that this amendment should be accepted with acclamation.[49]

It is important to know that the confabulations of the honourable MPs coincided with the second India–Pakistan war. This is likely to have triggered Mani's patriotic fervour and made him keen to counter Pakistan's portrayal of India. He wanted BHU to be renamed so that India may project its secularism and, it seems, assert moral superiority over its adversary.

As opinion in the upper house built up in favour of BHU's renaming, D. Thengari (1920–2004) and Prof. A.R. Wadia (1888–1971) struck a note of dissent and urged caution. A member of the Bharatiya Jana Sangh (BJS, henceforth only Jana Sangh), the former represented UP in the Rajya Sabha.[50] Addressing the house on 11 November, Thengari argued:

> [T]here is no case for changing the original name of the Banaras Hindu University. The term 'Hindu' is not denominational; it is national ... during the last five decades nobody could prove that the insertion of the word 'Hindu' had created any communalism in the Banaras Hindu University ... Secondly, even if it is taken for granted that all denominational names should be dropped, then it would be more appropriate to bring forward a separate bill banning all denominational titles of educational institutions, so that in one bill we achieve the purpose which is sought to

> be achieved. Thirdly, it would be more appropriate to allow the educational institutions themselves to decide what names they should adopt or should not adopt instead of … [the MPs] legislating on the point.[51]

In short, Thengari thought that there was nothing implicitly narrow about the term 'Hindu' and did not see the point in removing it from 'Banaras Hindu University'. Further, he wanted the government to be consistent in the way of secularism, as far as banning or allowing educational institutions from having denominational names was concerned.

Like his academic colleague, Dr Chand, Prof. Wadia was a nominated member of the Rajya Sabha.[52] On 16 November, he rose to express his 'personal concern over the change of the name'. Prof. Wadia thought that this was being done 'in a very revolutionary fashion'.The renaming, he indicated, did not augur well. Prof. Wadia told the house:

> [I] was in Banaras two days ago and … was very much depressed and distressed to learn that the whole Banaras city and the Banaras Hindu University are terribly agitated over the change of the name. They do not want a change in the name … and telegrams have already been sent to the President, the Prime Minister and the Education Minister… the civil and police authorities have been putting their heads together to prevent any untoward developments.

Prof. Wadia hoped (despite evidence to the contrary) that an agitation would not break out over the issue. He concluded by saying that he did not much like the new name because it was 'bound to be shortened to read "MMM"'.[53]

Thengari spoke on the bill a second time on 16 November. As he reported, the disaffection against the change of name was not restricted to BHU and Banaras city but appeared to be spreading across UP:

> [S]o far as the name is concerned, I may inform the hon. Education Minister that I had on the last Saturday and Sunday been to some parts of UP and really the people are agitated over the point, and I should request the hon. Education Minister to reconsider his decision of changing the name because the people have genuine affection and affinity for this particular name, particularly because, as I have said, the name, according to them denotes a national and not denominational sense.[54]

The Congress-dominated Rajya Sabha was in no mood to heed the pleas of Thengari and Prof. Wadia. It passed the bill without much further ado. In fact, the vote in its favour was nearly unanimous, with the Left—the Communist Party of India (CPI), the Praja Socialist Party (PSP), and the Samyukta Socialist Party (SSP)—combining with the Congress. Only two votes, both by the Jana Sangh, were cast against the bill in the upper house.[55] Thus, in the end, only Thengari and his fellow partyman, Vimal Kumar Chordia (1924–2019), a member of the Rajya Sabha from MP,[56] offered substantive opposition to the renaming of BHU. Somehow, even the conscientious Prof. Wadia fell in line behind the ruling party.

Agitation by BHU Students and Discussion in the Lok Sabha

BHU Students' Association began to rally against the bid to rename their university on 15 November. It conducted a meeting at the main gate of BHU and issued a ten-day 'ultimatum' to the government to reconsider the renaming. Failing this, BHU Students' Association declared itself free to take 'necessary action'. Further, students at the meeting vowed to make every possible sacrifice to preserve the original name of their institution.[57]

The Jana Sangh came to the active support of the agitating students soon after. It threw in its lot with the Action Committee of BHU Students' Association as it gave the call for a general boycott of classes in the university on 17 November (it would eventually drag on until 29 November). The Jana Sangh asked the people of Banaras to observe a complete suspension of business on this day. At the same time, students from other institutions lent their support to the BHU students' agitation. On the afternoon of 17 November, about 1,500 students from Kashi Vidyapith and Harish Chandra College, Banaras, marched through the city in unison with 3,000 BHU students. The youthful throng raised the battle cry *'Har Har Mahadev'* to the sound of gongs, bells, and conches.[58]

In the evening, an enormous crowd of about 10,000 gathered at a meeting organized by the Jana Sangh and the All-India Hindu Mahasabha around the Town Hall of Banaras. Speaking on the occasion, Jana Sangh leader, Harish Chandra Srivastava (1925–2015), resolved to launch a nationwide movement if the government did not rescind the renaming of BHU within the stipulated time. If required, he also threatened to mobilize 'one-crore [ten million] people' to surround the parliament building in Delhi. In the end, a resolution affirming the word 'Hindu' to be coterminous with Indian nationality and urging the government to retain it in 'Banaras Hindu University' was passed at the meeting.[59]

As the agitation grew increasingly impassioned and politicized, attempts were made to defuse it. For example, on 19 November, Raj Narayan (1917–86), Ugra Sen, and Prabhu Singh, all members of the SSP, appealed to BHU students to not 'press their demand' for the retention of 'Hindu' in the name of their institution. They advised that they withdraw the agitation while alleging that it owed to the 'connivance' of 'university officials, local administration and communal elements'.[60]

At the same time, the ruling party was making its own efforts to placate BHU students. M.C. Chagla received a small delegation of them on the very day the socialist leaders made their appeal. As reported by the daily, *The Hindustan Times*, he asked them to present their viewpoint before MPs and not resort to strikes and damage the name of their university. The students, on their part, 'strongly urged' that 'Hindu' in 'Banaras Hindu University' is not removed.[61]

The four-member delegation was received by Prime Minister, Lal Bahadur Shastri (1904–66), Home Minister, Gulzarilal Nanda (1898–1998), and Minster for Parliamentary Affairs, Satyanarayan Sinha (1900–83), the following day. They assured these youths that their demand would be conveyed to the Lok Sabha.[62] The exertions by the PM and his cabinet colleagues notwithstanding, it is likely that the delegation did not return very satisfied. As a result, the situation at BHU sharply deteriorated. Headlined 'Students control BHU area', a front-page report in *The Hindustan Times* described a campus on the boil. It pertained to 22 November:

> The strike in the Banaras Hindu University … took a serious turn when the students blocked the main gate of the university and took possession of one of the rooms of the chief proctor's office.
>
> The students … [were] fully in control of the main gate and nobody … [was] allowed to enter the university campus without furnishing detailed identity. Only those … [were] allowed inside the campus who … [wore] a black badge round their arms as a protest against the BHU Amendment Bill.
>
> The university authorities … locked the chief proctor's office and removed all staff from office as well as the main gate.
>
> …
>
> Meanwhile students from other cities of the State and from Bihar … arrived to take part in the agitation.[63]

In other words, a full-scale insurrection was underway at BHU. The university authorities had lost control, while the agitating students had received reinforcements from outside. It was almost as though the campus had been turned into some kind of liberated zone.

While the students' agitation rose to a fever pitch, certain prominent citizens stepped up to condemn the government's move. Dr C.P. Ramaswami Aiyar (1879–1966), Vice-Chancellor of Annamalai University, termed the removal of 'Hindu' from 'Banaras Hindu University' 'in the name of secularism' a dishonour to the name of Malaviya. The venerable savant thought that secularism 'did not mean the abolition of names'. He made these remarks while presiding over the silver jubilee celebrations of BHU Alumni Association in Madras on 21 November.[64] C. Rajagopalachari (1878–1972), the former

Governor-General of India, came out against the renaming of BHU on 23 November. He argued that 'names indicate the history of institutions'. Thus, Rajagopalachari trenchantly observed, Christian, Jain, or Vaishnava institutions could not be made to rename themselves, just as 'political leaders ... [could not] be asked to change their Hindu names in order to demonstrate their secularity'.[65]

The ruling party, on the other hand, was mellowing its stand and seemed to be looking for an escape route. Coincident with Rajagopalachari's remarks, Shastri and Chagla declared that the government had an 'open mind' (regarding the renaming of BHU) and did not consider itself 'bound by the Rajya Sabha's decision'.[66] Nevertheless, the anger of BHU students was not letting up. *The Hindu* newspaper reported the following situation at the university on 23 November:

> Banaras Hindu University students ... observed "Black Day" by hoisting black flags on the main gate of the University, the Chief Proctor's office and on some hostel buildings. They were controlling traffic passing through the main gate. Most of them wore black badges on their arms.

The Vice-Chancellor tried to bring the situation under control that evening by addressing the students. He urged them not to 'spoil their cause' and to 'desist from coercive and violent forms of agitation'. Bhagwati informed the irate lot that the 'B.H.U. Bill' would be the very first item on the Lok Sabha's agenda the following day.[67] He had, we imagine, put out feelers to the government and was given the assurance.

Chagla did not let Bhagwati down. Even though the lower house did not take up the 'B.H.U. Bill' first thing on 24 November, the Minister of Education ensured that discussion on it commenced shortly after noon. As he introduced the bill, Chagla told the Lok Sabha that it had been passed in the upper house 'by an overwhelming majority', with only two against votes. He was, it seems, trying to dispel any prejudice that might have accumulated against it on account of the goings on at BHU. Subsequently, he dwelt on the logic behind the move to rename the university. Repeating the argument he had made in the Rajya Sabha, he told the house that it was because BHU was a 'national institution, an all-India institution, and should not have a denominational name'. 'The second consideration,' said Chagla, 'was that the Banaras Hindu University owed its existence, its inspiration to Madan Mohan Malaviya.'[68] Hence, the government thought it fit to replace the name 'Banaras Hindu University' with 'Madan Mohan Malaviya Kashi Vishwavidyalaya'. Chagla emphasized, as he previously had in the upper house, that 'no disrespect whatever [sic] was intended to Hindus'.[69]

Chagla's glib persuasions ran into critical and chary reactions in the Lok Sabha. Dr M.S. Aney, for example, made the following remark as he wound up:

> I can understand we should not take into consideration the students' agitation. But why should we not take into consideration what is going on in the whole country against this?[70]

As we see it, the independent MP from the Nagpur constituency[71] (Maharashtra) resorted to some sarcasm against the Minister of Education. Apparently, considerable public opinion had built up across the country in favour the agitation at BHU. Dr Aney, as a result, urged prudence upon Chagla.

Another MP to do so was Dr L.M. Singhvi. An independent like Dr Aney, he represented the Jodhpur constituency (Rajasthan) in the lower house.[72] Dr Singhvi recommended the following course of action to Chagla:

> [I]n order that the temper on this whole thing may cool off, that a proper consideration of this whole matter may take place and that this House may be better able to gauge public opinion and to see the pros and cons of the whole situation, the hon. Minister himself should bring a motion before this house that this Bill be re-committed either to the Select Committee of this House or the Joint Committee of both the Houses … the Government has also to make up its mind in respect of such vital matters; it cannot abdicate its responsibility; it must come forward; it must review its stand.[73]

Dr Singhvi, as we understand, thought that the government ought to buy time and not move on the bill against the backdrop of an agitation and unfavourable public opinion. He also seemed to hint that, if required, the ruling party should not be averse to dropping the idea of renaming BHU altogether.

Certain MPs were frankly outspoken in their opposition to the Banaras Hindu University (Amendment) Bill. The Swatantra Party (SP) man Krishnapal Singh, as we discover, was in no mood to mince his words. Elected to the lower house from the Jalesar constituency[74] (UP), he announced himself to be 'vehemently opposed to any change in the existing name of the Banaras Hindu University'[75] and delivered the following polemic:

> Those who wish to introduce a change in the name of the university put forward arguments that the name 'Hindu' or

'Muslim' or any other such names in the names of certain institutions in our country would have some unfortunate and undesirable effect on the people or on products of these institutions. I say that this is contrary to what has actually happened. Especially, the Banaras Hindu University has produced some people who are known for their patriotism and for their nationalist views.

Secularism, even if we were a secular State, does not prevent people from following any religion they like, nor does it prevent them from having institutions as they like. I suppose in a secular state people are free to have the right to name their institution as they like; the Muslims are free to have a Muslim institution or call their institutions as Muslim institutions, Christians can name their own institutions as Christian institutions, and so on; I do not suppose these names will do any harm even to a secular State ... in a State or community which is multi-religious, and which believes intensely in religion, it will be very unfortunate if people did not the [sic.] freedom to call their institution in the manner they want it to be called. Therefore, this fear of the enthusiasts of secularism that the retention of the name ['Banaras Hindu University'] will bring in a conflict among communities is absolutely baseless. What we need is that we should see that all the communities live in harmony and that can only be done by a proper study of religion.

No religion teaches conflict. No religion wants that people should fight with one another. Therefore, I think, instead of discouraging the study of religion, we should encourage the study of religion.[76]

Singh, in brief, pointed out that, its denominational identity notwithstanding, BHU did not inculcate a parochial or communalist attitude. He also took the view that secularism must mean that no religion is hindered in any manner.

Thus, every religious group ought to have the right to establish its own institutions and give them explicitly denominational names. As Singh understood, this is in itself need not be the cause of friction or quarrels between adherents of different religions. On the contrary, he thought that denominational institutions would demonstrate how religions unite in advocating peace through systematic studies and provide a basis for social harmony.

Singh found a surprising ally in Ansar Harvani (1916–96). A Congressman, his Lok Sabha constituency was Bisauli (UP).[77] Harvani's position regarding the renaming of BHU was as follows:

> [S]ecularism does not mean banning the name 'Hindu' or 'Muslim'. Secularism means that in this country Hindus, Muslims, Parsis, Sikhs and every community will live in peace, will have equal right to develop and grow and to come to their own. Therefore I consider that too much insistence that the name of Banaras Hindu University should be changed is a sort of premature and infantile secularism. It is not that by changing the name of Banaras Hindu University we can change the character of the university: the character of the university will continue, whatever the name may be. There are in this country many kinds of institutions: Christian colleges are there, Sikh colleges are there, DAV [Dayanand Anglo-Vedic] colleges are there; a number of denominational institutions are there which have produced very good nationalists and very good patriots.... Therefore, I think we should see this question in that light and not think that by dropping the word 'Hindu' from the name of the Banaras Hindu University we will change the character of the university.... In this country there are many religions, communities and

> languages. All the communities, all the languages and all the religions should get equal opportunity to develop and enough opportunity to grow.[78]

Harvani's standpoint, in other words, was roughly the same as Singh's. In essence, he too argued that secularism entailed granting equal rights to all religious groups including the right to establish their own institutions. Quite acutely, he also exposed the needlessness of the endeavour to rename BHU by pointing out that an essentially Hindu institution would continue to be so even under an expediently non-denominational name.

Both Singh and Harvani were eventually outdone by Acharya J.B. Kripalani (1888–1982). He called out the ruling party for practising a selective secularism and scathingly denounced the Banaras Hindu University (Amendment) Bill. Remarkably, he did this despite being in the PSP. As we know, it had previously allied with the Congress to see the bill through the upper house. The conscientious MP, a former freedom fighter, from the Guna constituency (MP)[79], minced no words as he dwelt on the government's hypocrisy in community matters. As Kripalani pointed out, it was selectively targeting a Hindu institution for its denominational identity while being wary of reforming Muslim social usages:

> I think Mr Chagla was ill-advised to bring about this change in the name or to suggest this change in the name. What he should have done is to bring a Bill before parliament that all communal names must be abolished … this government does not enjoy the confidence of the people in certain matters, and in this one matter, in this communal

> matter, it has acted in the past in a way which makes its words unreliable. The illustration of this was given by the Hindu Code Bill. While the Hindu Code Bill was to reform the Hindu society, the Government refused to reform the Muslim society and they did a great injustice to the Muslim community, especially to our Muslim sisters, by keeping polygamy yet alive which has been abolished in Turkey and Pakistan even. Whenever the question of the Muslim minority comes, government becomes nervous.

Subsequently, Kripalani suggested this face-saving course to the Minister of Education:

> I say this bill, as it is, may for the time being should be abrogated and it need not appear as if we have yielded to any threat from the students … this impression … can be obliterated is a statement is made here that in future no denominational names would be put up on any school or university and if such names are used no grant from the Government will be given to such institutions.[80]

Thus, just as Thengari had previously done in the Rajya Sabha, Kripalani demanded that the ruling party espouse secularism with some consistency.

The Communist Party of India (CPI) member Hirendra Nath Mukerjee (1907–2004) and the independent Gauri Shanker Kakkar tried their best to shore up the Banaras Hindu University (Amendment) Bill through some enthusiastic partisanship.[81] Nevertheless, despite the interventions from these MPs from the Calcutta Northeast (West Bengal) and Fatehpur (UP) constituencies,[82] the overall mood in the Lok Sabha was rather unfavourable towards BHU's renaming on 24 November. When the house resumed discussing the matter the following day, the first to speak was Congressman P.R. Chakravarti. His position was somewhat redolent of Kripalani's. The MP from the Dhanbad constituency (Bihar)[83] suggested that the government, for the time being, desist from renaming BHU. Chakravarti found it inadvisable on account of the (apparently hostile) public mood and the ongoing students' agitation. He thought that trouble would be pre-empted if the government brought in a new bill renaming both BHU and the Aligarh Muslim University (AMU) sometime later. As we understand, Chakravarti, like Thengari and Kripalani, wanted it to be even-handed in enforcing secularism:

> My idea … [is] to emphasize … that when a particular issue confronts the people at large and especially when young minds are charged with emotion, animated as well as agitated the Government has to take a realistic stand.… In this context, unless we have that comprehensive Bill, covering both the Aligarh Muslim University and the Banaras Hindu University, this apprehension [regarding the current bill] will create trouble and unrest.[84]

Chakravarti was followed by Hari Vishnu Kamath (1907–82). A member of the PSP, he represented the Hoshangabad constituency (MP) in the Lok Sabha.[85] Quite remarkably, instead of addressing the house, Kamath advanced the motion that 'Further debate on the bill be adjourned'.[86] It was seconded by Frank Anthony (1908–83), a nominated Anglo-Indian member of the lower house.[87] Soon enough, the motion was put to vote by the Speaker, Sardar Hukum Singh (1938–2018).[88] It received 137 'Ayes' against 51 'Noes' and prevailed with an overwhelming majority.[89]

The Banaras Hindu University (Amendment) Bill, in this way, unexpectedly fell through in the Lok Sabha. This was an unambiguous victory for the agitating students and a major embarrassment for the government. The fact that certain MPs went so far as to defy their respective parties to scuttle BHU's attempted renaming amply indicates the extent of public anger against it. As a matter of fact, Singh might have shown that extra alacrity in entertaining Kamath's motion on account of this anger. He might also have been influenced by the compelling positions of Kripalani and Chakravarti. Being a Congressman, Singh, it is quite likely, was eager to give his party an expedient exit from a quixotic misadventure. Given an opportunity by the Speaker, the Lok Sabha too was quick to affirm the public mood. It made Kamath's motion a total triumph. BHU, as a result, retained its denominational identity. No subsequent Congress government at the Centre contemplated tempering with it again. The students' agitation at the university was eventually called off on 29 November.[90] Thus ended the most tumultuous episode in Indian higher academia post-independent.

Conclusion

There is no doubt that the metropole recast the colony in multiple ways and transformed the natives' habitus or social world. As the Nigerian novelist Chinua Achebe (1930–2013) poignantly depicts in *Things Fall Apart*, the colonial missionary and administrator viewed the local social and cultural practices with a callous disregard and worked to change them as per their own notions of civilization. These forceful intrusions into the natives' social world caused it to fracture and fragment ('fall apart') in ways that it would never again be as it was. The representatives of the metropole were indeed agents of cataclysmic change and harbingers of a painful 'modernity'. From a tiny tribal hamlet in West Africa to the enormous, bustling political, cultural, and economic centres of India and China, this was a prominent aspect of the colonial reality. One may, in this way, make a compelling postulation of 'coloniality'.[1]

However, unlike what seems to be suggested by Bayly, the colonized native was by no means only a passive observer or willing party to their recasting and transformation. There were certainly elements within every native society who were alacritous in giving up their own ways for the colonizers' and considered themselves 'civilized' and 'modern' for it. These elements also actively collaborated with the colonizers in the oppression of their own people.

In other words, sections of native societies, as far as possible, voluntarily abandoned their pre-colonial mentalité and ways of life, and sought co-optation into the colonial power structures. A case in point is the 'brown sahibs', or the Anglicized (sometimes Christianized too) elites of colonial India, who, as far as possible, modelled themselves after the white rulers.

Nevertheless, the vast bulk of colonized Asians and Africans, elite and non-elite alike, retained great amounts of their original social and cultural subjectivities, even if they superficially and selectively adopted some Western 'bodily practices' (dress and language).[2] It is on account of these subjectivities that, as argued in the Introduction, the Western-derived economic and political frameworks and social, cultural, and intellectual influences, were not replicated or absorbed in colonial India in toto. They were generally reworked through conscious or unconscious native agency and produced, as we may term it, a dialogic modernity. Both postcolonial scholarship (to the extent that I am familiar with it) and perceptions of coloniality resultantly err in not factoring in native agency.

The story of BHU's establishment and formative years, as related in this book, it may be plausibly argued, is also that of the deployment of Indian agency within a colonial framework, namely, that of higher education. In this way, a considerable portion of this book is about how a distinctly Indian and Hindu subjectivity modulated an aspect of colonialism and successfully expressed itself in an institutional form. We do not deny that this subjectivity was at times ambiguous and fractured. This is indicated by the lenient and non-coercive (in essence liberal) approach towards religious instruction and the friction between orthodoxy and reformism at BHU, as also the heteroglossia in *BHU Magazine*. However, it is the very ambiguities and fractures in the subjectivity represented by BHU that made it a purveyor of dialogic modernity and, ipso facto, a form of incremental and long-term pushback against colonialism.

If one were to resort to Gramscian terminology, BHU provides an instance of native agency resisting colonialism through a kind of 'war of position'[3], that is, a piecemeal subversion of its ideological hegemony within higher education. The BHU story indicates that anti-colonial struggle did not always take the form of armed action or vast and tumultuous mass mobilizations. Instead, this struggle seems to have been dominantly waged through fabrication of dialogic modernities and various wars of position by native agents who tenaciously refused to have their original subjectivities (even though their wholeness eroded) effaced by a Western-derived modernity or allow colonial frameworks to rigidly determine their social initiatives.

Both postcolonial scholarship and expositions of coloniality need take note of this historical reality in logical pursuit of their sympathy for the colonized. To be properly rounded off, they must document their struggles to retain and express their native subjectivities. The votaries of decoloniality too could examine the dialogic modernities and wars of position apprehensible in the colonial situations to advance a coherent and applicable agenda. Postcolonial societies cannot contest Western universalism today unless they are told about the means through which it was once sought to be done by their colonized forebears.

BHU ran afoul with Gandhi and the post-Independent Congress regime at the Centre, since they were both unable to fully comprehend the institution's implications. The former could not grasp that the university broke the continuum of colonial ideology by disrupting its hegemony in one of the most crucial areas of social activity, that of the systematic and institutionally structured instruction and skilling of young people. This is rather ironical considering that Antonio Gramsci, a contemporary, attributed the quality of 'war of position' to the Gandhian mass mobilizations in his *Prison Notebooks*.[4]

After Independence, the central government failed to understand the uniquely Indian iteration of modernity that BHU represented through its denominational identity. Neither did it apprehend the way this identity posed a challenge to Western universalism. As a result, the Congress regime became an agent of the same universalism with regards to the institution as it tried to bring it within the ambit of a rigidly Western, 'separation of church and state' (BHU being a public university), notion of secularism.

To be fair to Gandhi and Chagla, they were not equipped with the perspective that hindsight has lent us. Since we are able to do so, let us acknowledge the immense value that the BHU story contains for our postcolonial society and duly celebrate it. Among other things, this must involve ensuring that the university never again faces the kind of crisis it did six decades ago. Secularism as a manifestation of Western universalism is a difficult enough proposition. It is worse when its votaries are selective in applying it, as the Congress was in 1965.

Notes

Introduction

1 C.A. Bayly, *The Birth of the Modern World. 1780–1914. Global Connections and Comparisons* (Blackwell Publishing, 2004).

2 See Rabindranath Tagore, *Nationalism* (New Delhi: Niyogi Books, 2012).

3 See Mahatma Gandhi, *Hind Swaraj* (Delhi: Rajpal, 2017 [Eighth Reprint]).

4 Abanindranath Tagore (1871–1951) and Nandalal Bose (1882–1966) are a couple of examples.

Chapter 1: The Century before BHU: Education in Colonial India

1 The EIC set up its first 'factory', or warehouse, in Surat, Gujarat, in 1608.

2 Bernard S. Cohn, *Colonialism and Its Forms of Knowledge. The British in India* (Princeton, New Jersey: Princeton University Press, 1996), p. 5.

3 Ibid.

4 Thomas R. Trautmann, *Aryans and British India* (New Delhi: Yoda Press, 2004), p. 3.

5 Ibid., p. 30.

6 Ibid.

7 Ibid., p. 28.

8 Ibid., p. 29.

9 Ibid., p. 113.

10 The course was subsequently split, and its first two years came to be taught at the East India College after its establishment in 1806. Initially based in the Hertford Castle, it was later shifted to Haileybury from where it functioned until 1858, the year in which it ceased operations. The reasons behind the establishment of the institution, as given by Trautmann, are that the top Company brass wanted to control the appointment of the writers 'and collect large fees for doing so' and placate the Evangelical establishment which was worried about the 'bad effects of early exposure to India on the British youth'. Ibid., p. 114.

11 Ibid.

12 Saumya Dey, *Becoming Hindus and Muslims: Reading the Cultural Encounter in Bengal* (Delhi: Munshiram Manoharlal, 2015), p. 134.

13 Thomas Roebuck, *Annals of the College of Fort William* (Calcutta: Printed by Philip Pereira, at the Hindoostanee Press, 1819), p. 15.

14 A prominent Civil Servant in the EIC's administration, Sir Barlow was the acting Governor-General in India between the death of Lord Cornwallis (1738–1805) and the appointment of Lord Minto (1751–1814), from 1805 to 1807.

15 *Annals of the College of Fort William*, p. 17.

16 The term was coined by Michel Foucault. He defines it as the 'institutions, procedures, analyses, and reflections' through which a 'complex form of power' is applied upon a population. See Michel Foucault, *Power. Essential Works. 1954-84. Volume Three* (Penguin Random House, 1994), pp. 219–20.

17 Passed by the British Parliament, it chiefly addressed the problems arisen in the EIC's legal administration.

18 Syed Nurullah and J.P. Naik, *History of Education in India during the British Period* (Bombay, Calcutta, Madras, London: Macmillan & Co. Ltd., 1943), p. 47.

19 A phrase used by Jonathan Duncan. J.P. Naik and Syed Nurullah, *A Students' History of Education in India.* (Madras: Macmillan India Limited, 1992), p. 37.

20 Ibid.

21 Ibid., p. 36.

22 The EIC had been granted the monopoly right to trade with India under a royal charter which was periodically renewed by the British Parliament. It did so each time by passing a 'Charter Act'.

23 *History of Education in India during the British Period*, p. 46.

24 Ibid.

25 Dharampal. *Collected Writings. Volume III. The Beautiful Tree: Indigenous Indian Education in the Eighteenth Century* (Goa: Other India Press, 2000), p.19.

26 Ibid., p. 11.

27 Ibid., p. 10.

28 Ibid.

29 Ibid.

30 Ibid., p. 11.

31 Ibid.

32 *History of Education in India during the British Period*, p. 5.

33 Ibid., p. 8.

34 Ibid., p. 7.

35 Ibid., p. 9.

36 Ibid.

37 Ibid., p. 12.

38 *A Students' History of Education in India*, p. 14.

39 *The Beautiful Tree*, p. 267.

40 Ibid.

41 *History of Education in India during the British Period*, p. 2.

42 *The Beautiful Tree*, p. 270.

43 Ibid.

44 Ibid., p. 269.

45 Ibid., p. 272.

46 Ibid., p. 54.
47 *History of Education in India during the British Period*, p. 55.
48 Burke sat in the House of Commons for nearly three decades, from 1766 to 1794.
49 *The Parliamentary History of England from the Earliest Period to the Year 1803, Vol. XXIII* (London, 1814), p. 647.
50 *History of Education in India during the British Period*, p. 57.
51 Ibid.
52 Ibid., p. 58.
53 Ainslie Thomas Ambree, *Charles Grant and British Rule in India* (London: George Allen & Unwin Ltd., 1962), p. 145.
54 Ibid., p. 146.
55 Ibid., p. 142.
56 Ibid., p. 150.
57 This was an informal group of the adherents of the Church of England that originally emerged in Clapham, a town in the vicinity of London. The Clapham Sect was known for its opposition to slavery and its passion for propagating the gospel.
58 *History of Education in India during the British Period*, p. 60.
59 Ibid., p. 61.
60 Ibid., p. 62.
61 Ibid., p. 63.
62 *The Parliamentary Debates from the Year 1803 to the Present Time. Vol. XXII* (London: 1812), p. 913.
63 *The Parliamentary Debates from the Year 1803 to the Present Time. Vol. XXIII* (London: 1813), p. 355.
64 Ibid., p. 358.
65 *The Parliamentary Debates from the Year 1803 to the Present Time. Vol. XXV* (London: 1813), p. 227.
66 Ibid., p. 825.
67 *The Parliamentary Debates from the Year 1803 to the Present Time. Vol. XXVI* (London: 1813), p. 556.

68 Sekhar Bandyopadhyay, *From Plassey to Partition and After. A History of Modern India* (Hyderabad: Orient BlackSwan, 2022), p. 79.

69 *History of Education in India during the British Period*, p. 66.

70 Ibid.

71 Economic historians broadly identify three modes of colonial exploitation: mercantile, liberal or capitalist, and finance capitalist. See Bipan Chandra, *Essays on Colonialism* (Orient BlackSwan, 1999), Chapter Three, 'Colonialism, Stages of Colonialism and the Colonial State.' Also, Ellen Meiksins Wood, *The Origin of Capitalism. A Longer View* (London & New York: Verso, 2002), Chapter 7, 'The Origin of Capitalist Imperialism.' And Paul M. Sweezy, *The Theory of Capitalist Development. Principles of Marxian Political Economy* (Delhi: Aakar Books, 2016), Part Four, 'Imperialism.'

72 *A Students' History of Education in India*, p. 61.

73 *History of Education in India during the British Period*, p. 79.

74 *A Students' History of Education in India*, p. 61.

75 Sivanath Sastri, *History of the Brahmo Samaj. Vol. I* (Calcutta: Published by R. Chatterji, 1911), p. 57.

76 *History of Education in India during the British Period*, p. 75.

77 Ibid., p. 77.

78 *History of the Brahmo Samaj*, pp. 57–58.

79 Ibid., p. 57.

80 Ibid., p. 56.

81 Ibid., p. 58.

82 *History of Education in India during the British Period*, p. 91.

83 Ibid., p. 85.

84 Ibid., p. 86.

85 Ibid., p. 88.

86 Ibid., p. 92.

87 Ibid., p. 96.

88 Ibid., pp. 78–79.

89 *A Students' History of Education in India*, p. 66.
90 Ibid., p. 70.
91 H. Sharp, ed., *Selections from Educational Records. Part I. 1781–1839* (Calcutta: Superintendent Government Printing, 1920), p. 109.
92 Ibid., p. 110.
93 Ibid., pp. 110–11.
94 Ibid., p. 114.
95 Ibid., p. 109.
96 Ibid., p. 116.
97 See George D. Bearce, Jr., 'Lord Wiliam Bentinck: The Application of Liberalism to India' in *The Journal of Modern History*, Vol. 28, No. 3 (Sep., 1956), pp. 234–246.
98 *Selections from Educational Records. Part I. 1781–1839*, p. 116.
99 *A Students' History of Education in India*, p. 73.
100 Ibid., p. 74.
101 *History of Education in India during the British Period*, pp. 114–17. Lord Auckland was the Governor-General from 1836 to 1842.
102 Ibid., p. 154.
103 Ibid., p. 135.
104 Ibid., p. 146.
105 Ibid., p. 147.
106 Ibid., pp. 154–55.
107 Ibid., p. 157.
108 Ibid., p. 158.
109 The Board of Control oversaw the EIC's civil, military, and revenue affairs in India.
110 J.A. Richey, ed., *Selections from Educational Records. Part II. 1840–1859* (Calcutta: Superintendent Government Printing, 1922), p. 365.
111 Ibid., p. 368.
112 *History of Education in India during the British Period*, pp. 162–64.

113 Ibid., p. 168.
114 Ibid., pp. 188–89.
115 Ibid., p. 190.
116 Ibid., p. 204.
117 Ibid.
118 Ibid., p. 205.
119 Ibid., p. 209.
120 *The Beautiful Tree*, pp. 75–80.

Chaper 2: Madan Mohan Malaviya: A Hindu Educationist

1 Sitaram Chaturvedi, *Madan Mohan Malaviya* (Publications Division: Ministry of Information and Broadcasting. Government of India, 2014 [Reprint]), p. 1.
2 Ibid., p. 2.
3 Ibid., p. 3.
4 S.L. Gupta, *Pandit Madan Mohan Malaviya. A Socio-Political Study* (Allahabad: Chugh Publications, 1978), p. 2.
5 Ibid., p. 5.
6 Ibid., p. 2.
7 *Madan Mohan Malaviya*, p. 9.
8 *Pandit Madan Mohan Malaviya. A Socio-Political Study*, p. 3.
9 Ibid.
10 Ibid., p. 4.
11 Ibid.
12 Ibid., p. 7.
13 Ibid.
14 *Madan Mohan Malaviya*, pp. 31–32.
15 As described by A.O. Hume. See Jagannath Prasad Misra, *Madan Mohan Malaviya and the Indian Freedom Movement* (New Delhi: Oxford University Press, 2016), p. 7.
16 *Speeches and Writings of Madan Mohan Malaviya* (Madras: G.A. Natesan & Co.), p. 5.
17 *Madan Mohan Malaviya and the Indian Freedom Movement*, p. 7.

18 *Speeches and Writings of Madan Mohan Malaviya*, p. 6.
19 Ibid.
20 Ibid., p. 7.
21 Ram Bahadur Rai, ed., *The Collected Works of Madan Mohan Malaviya* (*CWMMM*). *Volume IV* (New Delhi: Publications Division, Ministry of Information and Broadcasting, Government of India, and Mahamana Malaviya Mission, 2023), p. 4. This was on 19 January.
22 Ibid., p. 11. On 7 April 1903.
23 *Madan Mohan Malaviya and the Indian Freedom Movement*, p. 27.
24 Ibid., p. 28.
25 Ibid.
26 Ibid.
27 Ram Bahadur Rai, ed., *CWMMM. Volume V* (New Delhi: Publications Division, Ministry of Information and Broadcasting, Government of India and Mahamana Malaviya Mission, 2023), p. 9. Malaviya spoke on the 'Press Bill' in the Imperial Legislative Council on 8 January.
28 Ibid., p. 12.
29 Ibid., p. 14.
30 *Madan Mohan Malaviya and the Indian Freedom Movement*, p. 30.
31 Ibid., p. 31.
32 Ram Bahadur Rai, ed., *CWMMM. Volume VI* (New Delhi: Publications Division, Ministry of Information and Broadcasting, Government of India and Mahamana Malaviya Mission, 2023), p. 43. This was on 20 March.
33 *Madan Mohan Malaviya and the Indian Freedom Movement*, p. 86.
34 Ibid., p. 89.
35 Ibid.
36 Ibid., p. 90.
37 Ibid., pp. 221–28.

38 Ram Bahadur Rai, ed., *CWMMM. Volume III* (New Delhi: Publications Division, Ministry of Information and Broadcasting, Government of India and Mahamana Malaviya Mission, 2023). 'Pandit M.M. Malaviya's Statement on Repression in India upto April 20, 1932,' p. 234.

39 Malaviya, according to Jagannath Prasad Misra, 'made a continuous effort … to impress upon the contending factions to evolve a middle course which could appeal to both sides.' *Madan Mohan Malaviya and the Indian Freedom Movement*, p. 17.

40 Ibid., pp. 121–23.

41 Ibid., p. 207.

42 *Pandit Madan Mohan Malaviya. A Socio-Political Study*, p. 6.

43 *Madan Mohan Malaviya and the Indian Freedom Movement*, p. 11.

44 Ram Bahadur Rai, ed., *CWMMM. Volume I* (New Delhi: Publications Division, Ministry of Information and Broadcasting, Government of India and Mahamana Malaviya Mission, 2023), p. 5.

45 Ibid., pp. 9–10. The Central Provinces correspond to today's Madhya Pradesh.

46 Ibid., p. 18.

47 Ibid., p. 20.

48 Ibid., p. 24.

49 Ibid., p. 25.

50 Ibid.

51 Ibid., p. 51.

52 Stephen R. King, *One Language Two Scripts. The Hindi Movement in Nineteenth Century North India.* (Bombay: Oxford University Press, 1994), p. 126.

53 *Madan Mohan Malaviya and the Indian Freedom Movement*, p. 5.

54 Ibid.

55 'Sacred Symbol as Mobilizing Ideology: The North Indian Search for a "Hindu" Community' in *Comparative Studies in Society and History*, Oct., 1980, Vol. 22, No. 4 (Oct., 1980), pp. 597–625. P. 608.

56 *Pandit Madan Mohan Malaviya. A Socio-Political Study*, p. 328.

57 Ibid., p. 329.

58 *Pandit Madan Mohan Malaviya. A Socio-Political Study*, p. 289.

59 Ibid., p. 293.

60 *Madan Mohan Malaviya and the Indian Freedom Movement*, p. 145.

61 Ibid., p. 148.

62 Ibid., p. 149.

63 Ibid., p. 150.

64 Ibid.

65 Ibid., p. 145.

66 Ram Bahadur Rai, ed., *CWMMM. Volume III*, p. 255. This note was issued in August 1934.

67 *Madan Mohan Malaviya and the Indian Freedom Movement*, p. 157.

68 Ibid., p. 150.

69 Ibid.

70 *Speeches and Writings of Madan Mohan Malaviya*, p. 115.

71 Ibid., p. 114.

72 S.K. Maitra, 'Mahamana Pandit Madan Mohan Malaviya,' in Nand Lal Singh, ed., *Mahamana Malaviyaji Birth Centenary Commemoration Volume 25 December 1961* (Varanasi: Published by the Secretary, All-India Malaviyaji Centenary Celebration Committee, Banaras Hindu University), p. 93. Maitra terms Banaras Hindu University 'a glorious example of the mixture of idealism and realism'.

73 *CWMMM. Volume III*, p. 29.

74 Ibid.

75 Ibid., p. 38.

76 Ram Bahadur Rai, ed., *CWMMM. Volume V* (New Delhi: Publications Division, Ministry of Information and Broadcasting, Government of India and Mahamana Malaviya Mission, 2023), p. 37.

77 Ibid., p. 38.

78 Ibid., p. 40.

79 Ibid., p. 41.

80 Ibid., pp. 42–43.

81 Ram Bahadur Rai, ed., *CWMMM. Volume VI* (New Delhi: Publications Division, Ministry of Information and Broadcasting, Government of India and Mahamana Malaviya Mission, 2023), p. 16. The resolution had been moved by a certain Dr M.N. Banerjee.

82 Ram Bahadur Rai, ed., *CWMMM. Volume VIII* (New Delhi: Publications Division, Ministry of Information and Broadcasting, Government of India and Mahamana Malaviya Mission, 2023), p. 211. This was on 10 March 1920.

83 Ram Bahadur Rai, ed., *CWMMM. Volume II* (New Delhi: Publications Division, Ministry of Information and Broadcasting, Government of India and Mahamana Malaviya Mission, 2023), p. 73.

84 *Speeches and Writings of Madan Mohan Malaviya*, pp. 89–90. Malaviya made these remarks while delivering his presidential address at the annual session of the Congress in 1909.

85 Ram Bahadur Rai, ed., *CWMMM. Volume VII* (New Delhi: Publications Division, Ministry of Information and Broadcasting, Government of India and Mahamana Malaviya Mission, 2023), pp. 206–07. This was on 11 September 1919.

86 Leah Renold, *A Hindu Education. Early Years of the Banaras Hindu University* (New Delhi: Oxford University Press, 2005), p. 2.

87 Ibid., p. 3.

88 Kenneth W. Jones, *Arya Dharam. Hindu Consciousness in 19th-Century Punjab* (Delhi: Manohar, 1976), p. 68.
89 *A Hindu Education*, p. 3.
90 Ibid.
91 Sunita Singh, *Educational Philosophy of Madan Mohan Malaviya* (New Delhi: Atlantic Publishers & Distributors, 2022), p. 148.
92 S.L. Dar and S. Somaskandan, *History of the Banaras Hindu University* (Banaras Hindu University, 2007 [Reprint]), p. 48.
93 Ibid.
94 Ibid., pp. 43–44.
95 Ibid., p. 48.
96 Sumit Sarkar, *The Swadeshi Movement in Bengal. 1903–1908* (New Delhi: People's Publishing House, 1994 [Second Reprint]), p. 161. These leaders mooted the idea of a national university at a public meeting in the Field and Academy Club grounds in Calcutta on 24 October 1905.
97 Ram Bahadur Rai, ed., *CWMMM. Volume IX* (New Delhi: Publications Division, Ministry of Information and Broadcasting, Government of India and Mahamana Malaviya Mission, 2023), p. 2.
98 Ibid., p. 3.
99 Ibid., p. 4.
100 Ibid., p. 18.
101 Ibid., p. 19.
102 Ibid.
103 Ibid., p. 21.
104 Ibid., p. 22.
105 Ibid., p. 23.
106 Ibid., p. 24.
107 Ibid., p. 43.
108 Ibid., p. 42.
109 Ibid., p. 43.
110 Ibid, pp. 43–44.

111 Ibid., p. 43. The Mahasabha comprised eminent Sadhus, Shastris, and representatives of the Hindu community from all over India.

112 Ibid., pp. 44–45.

113 *Madan Mohan Malaviya and the Indian Freedom Movement*, p. 43.

114 Dar, S.L. and S. Somaskandan. 2007. *History of the Banaras Hindu University*. Banaras Hindu University, p. 84.

Chapter 3: BHU: The Inception (1911–15)

1 S.L. Dar and S. Somaskandan, *History of the Banaras Hindu University* (Banaras Hindu University, 2007 [Reprint]), p. 86.

2 See Annie Besant, *India: A Nation. A Plea for Indian Self-Government* (London, Edinburgh, New York: Dodge Publishing Co.) and Bipin Chandra Pal, *Mrs. Annie Besant* (Madras: Ganesh & Co. Publishers).

3 *History of the Banaras Hindu University*, p. 88.

4 Ibid., p. 89.

5 Ibid.

6 Ibid., p. 90.

7 Ibid., p. 101.

8 Ibid., pp. 90–91.

9 Ibid., p. 91.

10 Ibid.

11 Ibid., p. 101.

12 Ibid. Also see Parmanand, *Mahāmanā Madan Mohan Malaviya (An Historical Biography) Vol. I* (Banaras Hindu University, Malaviya Adhyayan Sansthan, 1985), p. 196.

13 *History of the Banaras Hindu University*, p. 103.

14 Jagannath Prasad Misra, *Madan Mohan Malaviya and the Indian Freedom Movement* (New Delhi: Oxford University Press, 2016), p. 46.

15 In a letter to the Private Secretary of the Lt. Governor of the United Provinces. See Ram Bahadur Rai, ed., *CWMMM*.

Volume IX (New Delhi: Publications Division, Ministry of Information and Broadcasting, Government of India and Mahamana Malaviya Mission, 2023), p. 52.

16 *History of the Banaras Hindu University*, p. 101.

17 *CWMMM. Volume IX*, p. 54.

18 Ibid., p. 58.

19 *Mahāmanā Madan Mohan Malaviya*, p. 199.

20 Ibid., p. 196.

21 *Madan Mohan Malaviya and the Indian Freedom Movement*, p. 47.

22 *CWMMM. Volume IX*, p. 65.

23 Ibid., p. 68.

24 Ibid., p. 69.

25 Ibid., p. 70.

26 Ibid., p. 71.

27 *History of the Banaras Hindu University*, p. 109. This announcement encapsulated his discussion with the members of the Central Hindu College Committee.

28 Ibid.

29 Ibid., p. 110.

30 Ibid. The date on which the *Advocate* caried the letter is not mentioned.

31 *CWMMM. Volume IX*, p. 80.

32 Ibid., p. 81.

33 Ibid., p. 82.

34 Ibid.

35 Ibid., p. 83.

36 Ibid., pp. 83–84.

37 Ibid., p. 86.

38 Ibid., p. 87.

39 Ibid.

40 Ibid., p. 89.

41 Ibid., p. 90.

42 Ibid., p. 91.

43 Ibid., p. 91.
44 Ibid., p. 92
45 Ibid.
46 Ibid., p. 102.
47 Ibid., p. 103.
48 He was crowned Emperor of India on the occasion.
49 *Mahāmanā Madan Mohan Malaviya*, p. 198.
50 Ibid., p. 205.
51 Ibid.
52 *CWMMM*. Volume IX, p. 160.
53 Ibid., p. 162.
54 Ibid., pp. 163–64.
55 Ibid., p. 165.
56 Ibid., p. 166.
57 Ibid., p. 167.
58 Ibid.
59 Ibid., p. 168.
60 Ibid., p. 169.
61 Ibid., p. 169.
62 Ibid., p. 170.
63 Ibid., p. 169.
64 Ibid., p. 170.
65 Ibid., p. 171.
66 Ibid.
67 Tejakar Jha, *The Inception of Banaras Hindu University: Who Was the Founder in the Light of Historical Documents?* (Partridge India, 2015), p. 7.
68 Ibid.
69 Ibid., p. 9.
70 Ibid., p. 172.
71 Ibid., p. 173.
72 Ibid., p. 175. Also, *Mahāmanā Madan Mohan Malaviya*, p. 204.
73 *History of the Banaras Hindu University*, p. 195.

74 *Mahāmanā Madan Mohan Malaviya*, pp. 204–05.
75 Ibid., p. 205.
76 *History of the Banaras Hindu University*, p. 199.
77 Ibid., p. 200.
78 *Mahāmanā Madan Mohan Malaviya*, p. 205.
79 Ibid., p. 206.
80 *The Inception of Banaras Hindu University*, p. 29.
81 Ibid., pp. 30–34.
82 *History of the Banaras Hindu University*, p. 210.
83 *Mahāmanā Madan Mohan Malaviya*, p. 207.
84 Ibid., p. 208.
85 Ibid., p. 209.
86 Ibid.
87 Ibid., p. 210.
88 Ibid., p. 211.
89 Ibid. Malaviya and Rameshwar Singh were accompanied by Pandit Din Dayalu Sharma, Babu Mangala Prasad (Joint Secretary, HUS), and Bhatele Shyam Behari (*CWMMM. Volume IX*, p. 199).
90 Ibid., p. 214.
91 *The Inception of Banaras Hindu University*, p. 37.
92 Ibid., pp. 37–38.
93 Ibid., p. 38.
94 Ibid., p. 39.
95 Ibid., p. 40.
96 Ibid., pp. 44–45.
97 *Mahāmanā Madan Mohan Malaviya*, pp. 215–16. The once-popular tradition that the Nagwa site was donated for Banaras Hindu University by the Maharaja of Banaras, Prabhu Narayan Singh (1855–1931), is untrue.
98 Ibid., p. 216.
99 Ibid., p. 219.
100 Ibid., p. 220.
101 Ibid., p. 218.

102 Ibid., p. 220.
103 *History of the Banaras Hindu University*, p. 212. This was in 1912.
104 Ibid., p. 218. Italics in original.
105 Ibid., p. 251.
106 *CWMMM. Volume IX*, pp. 273–74.
107 Ibid., pp. 275–76.
108 Ibid.
109 Ibid., p. 277.
110 Ibid.
111 Ibid., p. 279.
112 Ibid., pp. 279–80.
113 Ibid., p. 280.
114 Ibid., p. 296.
115 Ibid., p. 297.
116 Ibid., p. 297.
117 Ibid., pp. 300–33.

Chapter 4: BHU: The Making of an Institution (1916–47)

1 Parmanand, *Mahāmanā Madan Mohan Malaviya (An Historical Biography) Vol. I* (Banaras Hindu University, Malaviya Adhyayan Sansthan, 1985), p. 232.
2 S.L. Dar and S. Somaskandan, *History of the Banaras Hindu University* (Banaras Hindu University, 2007 [Reprint]), p. 376.
3 *Mahāmanā Madan Mohan Malaviya*, p. 232.
4 Ibid.
5 *History of the Banaras Hindu University*, p. 335.
6 Tejakar Jha, *The Inception of Banaras Hindu University: Who Was the Founder in the Light of Historical Documents?* (Partridge India, 2015), pp. 82–83.
7 Ibid., pp. 81–82.
8 *Mahāmanā Madan Mohan Malaviya*, p. 233.
9 *The Inception of Banaras Hindu University*, p. 83.

10 Ibid., p. 84.
11 Ibid., p. 85.
12 Ibid.
13 Ibid., p. 88.
14 Ibid., pp. 88–89.
15 Ibid., p. 90.
16 Ibid., p. 92.
17 *Mahāmanā Madan Mohan Malaviya*, p. 233.
18 Ibid., p. 234.
19 *History of the Banaras Hindu University*, p. 355.
20 Ibid., p. 358.
21 Ibid., p. 355.
22 Ibid., p. 362.
23 Ibid., p. 355.
24 Ibid.
25 Ibid., p. 364.
26 *Mahāmanā Madan Mohan Malaviya*, p. 237.
27 *History of the Banaras Hindu University*, p. 355.
28 *Mahāmanā Madan Mohan Malaviya*, p. 237.
29 Ibid., p. 238.
30 Ibid.
31 Ibid.
32 Ibid., p. 239.
33 Ibid., p. 240.
34 Ibid., pp. 426–27.
35 Ibid., pp. 429–30.
36 *History of the Banaras Hindu University*, pp. 490–91.
37 *Mahāmanā Madan Mohan Malaviya*, p. 432.
38 Ibid., p. 431.
39 Ibid., pp. 432–33.
40 Ibid., p. 439.
41 Ibid., p. 508.
42 Ibid., pp. 509–10.
43 Ibid., pp. 511–13.

44 Ram Bahadur Rai, ed., *CWMMM. Volume X* (New Delhi: Publications Division, Ministry of Information and Broadcasting, Government of India and Mahamana Malaviya Mission, 2023), p. 139.
45 Ibid., p. 143.
46 Ibid., p. 144.
47 Ibid.
48 Ibid., p. 147.
49 *Mahāmanā Madan Mohan Malaviya*, pp. 513–19.
50 *History of the Banaras Hindu University*, p. 410.
51 Ibid., p. 411.
52 Ibid., p. 413.
53 Leah Renold, *A Hindu Education. Early Years of the Banaras Hindu University* (New Delhi: OUP, 2005), p. 162.
54 Ibid., p. 163. The *Central Hindu College Magazine* was renamed and restarted as the *BHU Magazine* in 1925. The publication would later be called the *Journal of BHU* (Ibid., p. 165).
55 Ibid., p. 163.
56 Ibid., p. 166.
57 See 'Discourse in the Novel' in Michael Holquist, ed., Caryl Emerson and Michael Holquist, trans., *The Dialogic Imagination. Four Essays by M.M. Bakhtin* (New Delhi: Pinnacle Learning, 2014).
58 *A Hindu Education*, p. 159.
59 Ibid.
60 *History of the Banaras Hindu University*, p. 635.
61 *A Hindu Education*, p. 160.
62 Ibid., p. 161.
63 Ibid., p. 159.
64 Ibid., pp. 148–49.
65 Ibid., p. 149.
66 Ibid., p. 148.
67 Ibid., p. 144.

68 Ibid., p. 154.
69 Ibid., p. 133.
70 *Sanātana Dharma. An Advanced Text-Book of Hindu Religion and Ethics* (Adyar, Madras: The Theosophical Publishing House, 1940), p. x.
71 Ibid., p. vii.
72 See 'Contents.' Ibid., pp. 11–12.
73 *A Hindu Education*, p. 134.
74 Ibid.
75 Ibid., p. 135.
76 Ibid., p. 136.
77 Ibid.
78 *History of the Banaras Hindu University*, p. 416.
79 Ibid., p. 417.
80 Ibid., p. 475.
81 Ibid., p. 477.
82 Ibid., p. 481.
83 Ibid., pp. 479–80.
84 Ibid., p. 480.
85 Ibid., p. 482.
86 *A Hindu Education*, p. 126.
87 *History of the Banaras Hindu University*, p. 742.
88 *A Hindu Education*, p. 152.
89 Ibid., p.183.
90 Ibid., p. 177.
91 Ibid., p. 152.
92 Ibid., p. 153.
93 Ibid., p. 190.
94 For a fuller elaboration of the concept, see Sandria B. Freitag, *Collective Action and Community. Public Arenas and the Emergence of Communalism in North India* (Delhi: OUP, 1990).
95 *A Hindu Education*, p. 191.
96 *History of the Banaras Hindu University*, p. 556.

97 Ibid., p. 557.
98 Ibid., p. 742.
99 Ibid., p. 425.
100 Ibid., p. 456.
101 Ibid., p. 463.
102 Ibid., p. 549.
103 Ibid., p. 551.
104 Ibid., p. 553.
105 Ibid., p. 554.
106 Ibid., p. 555.
107 Ibid., p. 741.
108 Ibid., p. 636.
109 Ibid., p. 637.
110 Ibid., p. 745.
111 Ibid., p. 639.
112 Ibid., p. 752.
113 *A Hindu Education*, pp. 170–75.
114 Ibid., p. 200.
115 Ibid., p. 204.
116 *History of the Banaras Hindu University*, p. 538.
117 *A Hindu Education*, p. 88.
118 Ibid.
119 Ibid., p. 86.
120 Ibid., pp. 88–89.
121 *History of the Banaras Hindu University*, p. 530.
122 Ibid., p. 614.
123 Ibid., p. 621.
124 Ibid., p. 715.
125 Ibid., p. 717.

Chapter 5: BHU after Independence: Assault upon Identity (1948–65)

1 This professorship was created in 1936 with a grant from the Spalding Trust with the objective of promoting greater

understanding between the world religions. Radhakrishnan was the first to be appointed to it.

2 S.L. Dar and S. Somaskandan, *History of the Banaras Hindu University* (Banaras Hindu University, 2007 [Reprint]), pp. 743–44.
3 Ibid., p. 749.
4 Ibid., p. 751.
5 Ibid., p. 754.
6 Ibid., pp. 754–55.
7 Ibid., p. 757.
8 Ibid., pp. 769–72.
9 Ibid., p. 784.
10 Ibid., pp. 785–86.
11 Ibid., p. 786.
12 Ibid., p. 808.
13 Ibid., pp. 816–19.
14 Ibid., p. 820.
15 Ibid., pp. 826–27.
16 Ibid., p. 828.
17 Ibid., p. 840.
18 Ibid., p. 843.
19 Ibid., p. 779.
20 Ibid., pp. 844–45.
21 Ibid., pp. 859–62.
22 Ibid., pp. 849–50.
23 Ibid., p. 856.
24 Ibid., p. 863.
25 Ibid., p. 766.
26 Ibid., p. 767.
27 Ibid., pp. 846–47.
28 Ibid., pp. 847–48.
29 Ibid., pp. 764–65.
30 Ibid., pp. 837–39.
31 Ibid., p. 775.

32 Ibid., p. 780.
33 Ibid., pp. 786–91.
34 Ibid., p. 803.
35 Ibid., pp. 834–35.
36 Chagla was a member of the Rajya Sabha from Maharashtra. *Rajya Sabha Members Biographical Sketches. 1952-2019* (New Delhi: Rajya Sabha Secretariat), p. 98.
37 *Parliamentary Debates. Rajya Sabha. Official Reports, Vol. LIV, No. 1* (New Delhi: Rajya Sabha Secretariat), column no. 1283.
38 Ibid., column nos. 1571–72.
39 *Rajya Sabha Members Biographical Sketches. 1952–2019*, p. 2.
40 *Parliamentary Debates. Rajya Sabha. Official Reports, Vol. LIV, No. 1*, column nos. 797–98.
41 *Rajya Sabha Members Biographical Sketches. 1952–2019*, p. 415.
42 *Parliamentary Debates. Rajya Sabha. Official Reports, Vol. LIV, No. 1*, column nos. 826–27.
43 *Rajya Sabha Members Biographical Sketches. 1952–2019*, p. 522.
44 *Parliamentary Debates. Rajya Sabha. Official Reports, Vol. LIV, No. 1*, column no. 859.
45 Ibid., column no. 860.
46 *Rajya Sabha Members Biographical Sketches. 1952*–2019, p. 522.
47 *Parliamentary Debates. Rajya Sabha. Official Reports, Vol. LIV, No. 1*, column no. 989.
48 *Rajya Sabha Members Biographical Sketches. 1952*–2019, p. 275.
49 *Parliamentary Debates. Rajya Sabha. Official Reports, Vol. LIV, No. 1*, column no. 1286.
50 *Rajya Sabha Members Biographical Sketches. 1952*–2019, p. 529.
51 *Parliamentary Debates. Rajya Sabha. Official Reports, Vol. LIV, No. 1*, column nos. 994–95.
52 *Rajya Sabha Members Biographical Sketches. 1952*–2019, p. 558.
53 *Parliamentary Debates. Rajya Sabha. Official Reports, Vol. LIV, No. 1*, column nos. 1540–41.
54 Ibid., column no. 1546.

55 Anil Baran Ray and Anil Baran Rai, 'Secularism and Political Protest: The Case of Banaras Hindu University (BHU) Students' Agitation of 1965' in *The Indian Journal Of Political Science*, Oct–Dec. 1978, Vol. 39, No. 4 (Oct–Dec. 1978), pp. 620–23. P.621.
56 *Rajya Sabha Members Biographical Sketches. 1952*–2019, p. 115.
57 'Secularism and Political Protest: The Case of Banaras Hindu University (BHU) Students', *The Indian Journal Of Political Science*, Oct–Dec. 1978, Vol. 39, No. 4 (Oct–Dec. 1978), p. 624.
58 Ibid., p. 625.
59 Ibid., p. 626.
60 *The Hindustan Times*, 20 November 1965, p. 8 (New Delhi: Pradhan Mantri Museum and Library, microfilm R-2538).
61 Ibid.
62 *The Hindustan Times*, 21 November 1965, p. 9 (New Delhi: Pradhan Mantri Museum and Library, microfilm R-2538).
63 *The Hindustan Times*, 23 November 1965, p. 1 (New Delhi: Pradhan Mantri Museum and Library, microfilm R-2538).
64 *The Hindu*, 22 November 1965, p. 9 (New Delhi: Pradhan Mantri Museum and Library, microfilm R-8340).
65 *The Hindustan Times*, 24 November 1965, p. 4 (New Delhi: Pradhan Mantri Museum and Library, microfilm R-2538).
66 *The Hindustan Times*, 24 November 1965, p. 1 (New Delhi: Pradhan Mantri Museum and Library, microfilm R-2538).
67 *The Hindu*, 24 November 1965, p. 1 (New Delhi: Pradhan Mantri Museum and Library, microfilm R-8340).
68 *Lok Sabha Debates (Thirteenth Session), Third Series Vol., XLVIII-No. 15* (New Delhi: Lok Sabha Secretariat), column no. 3618.
69 Ibid., column no. 3619.
70 Ibid., column no. 3620.
71 Digital Sansad. List of Members (htttp://sansad.in/Is/members). Accessed on 18 August 2024.

72 Ibid. Accessed on 18 August 2024.

73 *Lok Sabha Debates (Thirteenth Session), Third Series Vol., XLVIII-No. 15*, column no. 3631.

74 Digital Sansad. List of Members (htttp://sansad.in/Is/members). Accessed on 20 August 2024.

75 *Lok Sabha Debates (Thirteenth Session), Third Series Vol., XLVIII-No. 15*, column no. 3635.

76 Ibid., column nos. 3636–37.

77 Digital Sansad. List of Members (htttp://sansad.in/Is/members). Accessed on 20 August 2024.

78 Ibid., column no. 3677.

79 Digital Sansad. List of Members (htttp://sansad.in/Is/members). Accessed on 21 August 2024.

80 *Lok Sabha Debates (Thirteenth Session), Third Series Vol., XLVIII-No. 15*, column nos. 3701–02.

81 Ibid., column nos. 3647–51 and 3716–20.

82 Digital Sansad. List of Members (htttp://sansad.in/Is/members). Accessed on 21 August 2024.

83 Ibid., Accessed on 23 August 2024. This is before the creation of the Jharkhand state when Dhanbad was part of Bihar.

84 *Lok Sabha Debates (Thirteenth Session), Third Series Vol., XLVIII-No. 16* (New Delhi: Lok Sabha Secretariat), column nos. 3863–64.

85 Digital Sansad. List of Members (htttp://sansad.in/Is/members). Accessed on 23 August 2024.

86 *Lok Sabha Debates (Thirteenth Session), Third Series Vol., XLVIII-No. 16*, column no. 3866.

87 Ibid., column no. 3867.

88 His Lok Sabha constituency was Patiala (Punjab).

89 *Lok Sabha Debates (Thirteenth Session), Third Series Vol., XLVIII-No. 16*, column no. 3873.

90 *The Hindu*, 30 November 1965, p. 4 (New Delhi: Pradhan Mantri Museum and Library, microfilm R-8340).

Conclusion

1 For greater elaboration of the concept see J. Sai Deepak, *India That Is Bharat: Coloniality, Civilization, Constitution* (Delhi: Bloomsbury India, 2021).

2 I have borrowed the phrase with its implications from C.A. Bayly. See *The Birth of the Modern World, 1780–1914. Global Connections and Comparisons* (Blackwell Publishing, 2004).

3 Antonio Gramsci (1891–1937) was an Italian Marxist. 'War of movement' and 'war of position' are concepts developed by him to describe different types of conflict. The former is armed warfare, while the latter occurs 'on the terrain of politics'. 'War of position' may be understood as parties contending for hegemony in the overall civil society space. See Quintin Hoare and Geoffrey Nowell Smith, ed. & trans., *Selections from the Prison Notebooks of Antonio Gramsci* (New York: International Publishers, 1992 [eleventh reprint]), p. 229.

4 Ibid.

Bibliography

Primary Sources

Biographical Records

Rajya Sabha Secretariat. 2019. *Rajya Sabha Members Biographical Sketches: 1952–2019* New Delhi: Rajya Sabha Secretariat.

Digital Sansad. 'List of Members'. Retrieved from: http://sansad.in/Is/members

British Parliamentary Debates

Great Britain Parliament. 1812. *The Parliamentary Debates from the Year 1803 to the Present Time (Vol. XXII).* London: T.C. Hansard.

Great Britain Parliament. 1813. *The Parliamentary Debates from the Year 1803 to the Present Time (Vol. XXIII).* London: T.C. Hansard.

Great Britain Parliament. 1813. *The Parliamentary Debates from the Year 1803 to the Present Time (Vol. XXV).* London: T.C. Hansard.

Great Britain Parliament. 1813. *The Parliamentary Debates from the Year 1803 to the Present Time (Vol. XXVI).* London: T.C. Hansard.

Great Britain Parliament. 1814. *The Parliamentary History of England from the Earliest Period to the Year 1803 (Vol. XXIII).* London: T.C. Hansard.

Lok Sabha and Rajya Sabha Debates

Lok Sabha Debates (Thirteenth Session), Third Series, XLVIII (15). New Delhi: Lok Sabha Secretariat.

Lok Sabha Debates (Thirteenth Session), Third Series, XLVIII (16). New Delhi: Lok Sabha Secretariat.

Parliamentary Debates: Rajya Sabha (Official Reports), LIV (1). New Delhi: Rajya Sabha Secretariat.

Published Archival Material

Richey, J.A. (ed.). 1922. *Selections from Educational Records: Part II (1840–59)*. Calcutta: Superintendent Government Printing.

Roebuck, T. 1819. *Annals of the College of Fort William*. Calcutta: Hindoostanee Press.

Sharp, H. (ed.). 1920. *Selections from Educational Records: Part I (1781–1839)*. Calcutta: Superintendent Government Printing.

Published Speeches and Letters of Madan Mohan Malaviya, Maharaja of Darbhanga, and Harcourt Butler

Jha, T. 2015. *The Inception of Banaras Hindu University: Who Was the Founder in the Light of Historical Documents?* India: Partridge India.

Rai, R.B. (ed.). 2023. *Collected Works of Madan Mohan Malaviya* (*CWMMM*), *Volumes I-X*. New Delhi: Publications Division, Ministry of Information and Broadcasting, Government of India, and Mahamana Malaviya Mission.

Speeches and Writings of Madan Mohan Malaviya. Madras: G.A. Natesan & Co.

Tracts and Polemics

Besant, A. *India: A Nation. A Plea for Indian Self-Government*. London, Edinburgh, New York: Dodge Publishing Co.

Besant, A. 1940. *Sanātana Dharma: An Advanced Text-Book of Hindu Religion and Ethics*. Adyar, Madras: The Theosophical Publishing House.

Gandhi, M. 2017. *Hind Swaraj*. Delhi: Rajpal.

Tagore, R. 2012. *Nationalism*. New Delhi: Niyogi Books.

Newspapers

The Hindu. 22–30 November 1965. New Delhi: Pradhan Mantri Museum and Library.

The Hindustan Times. 20–24 November 1965. New Delhi: Pradhan Mantri Museum and Library.

Secondary Sources

Journal Articles and Book Chapters

Bakhtin, M.M. 2014. 'Discourse in the Novel'. *The Dialogic Imagination: Four Essays by M.M. Bakhtin*, edited by M. Holquist and translated by C. Emerson and M. Holquist. New Delhi: Pinnacle Learning.

Ray, A.B. 1978. 'Secularism and Political Protest: The Case of Banaras Hindu University (BHU) Students' Agitation of 1965'. *The Indian Journal of Political Science*, 39(4), pp. 620–23.

Bearce, G.D. Jr. 1956. 'Lord Wiliam Bentinck: The Application of Liberalism to India'. *The Journal of Modern History*, 28(3), pp. 234–46.

Freitag, S. 1980. 'Sacred Symbol as Mobilizing Ideology: The North Indian Search for a "Hindu" Community'. *Comparative Studies in Society and History*, 22(4), pp. 597–625.

Maitra, S.K. 1961. 'Mahamana Pandit Madan Mohan Malaviya'. *Mahamana Malaviyaji Birth Centenary Commemoration*. Varanasi: All-India Malaviyaji Centenary Celebration Committee, Banaras Hindu University.

Books

Ambree, A.T. 1962. *Charles Grant and British Rule in India*. London: George Allen & Unwin Ltd.

Bandyopadhyay, S. 2022. *From Plassey to Partition and After: A History of Modern India*. Hyderabad: Orient BlackSwan.

Bayly, C.A. 2004. *The Birth of the Modern World (1780–1914): Global Connections and Comparisons*. Blackwell Publishing.

Chandra, B. 1999. *Essays on Colonialism*. Hyderabad: Orient BlackSwan.

Chaturvedi, S. *Madan Mohan Malaviya*. New Delhi: Ministry of Information.

Cohn, B.S. 1996. *Colonialism and its Forms of Knowledge: The British in India*. Princeton, New Jersey: Princeton University Press.

Dar, S.L. and S. Somaskandan. 2007. *History of the Banaras Hindu University*. Banaras Hindu University.

Deepak, J.S. 2021. *India That Is Bharat: Coloniality, Civilization, Constitution*. Delhi: Bloomsbury India.

Dey, S. 2015. *Becoming Hindus and Muslims: Reading the Cultural Encounter in Bengal*. Delhi: Munshiram Manoharlal.

Dharampal. 2000. *The Beautiful Tree: Indigenous Indian Education in the Eighteenth Century*. Goa: Other India Press.

Foucault, M. 1994. *Power: Essential Works (1954–84; Volume Three)*. Penguin Random House.

Freitag, S.B. 1990. *Collective Action and Community: Public Arenas and the Emergence of Communalism in North India*. Delhi: Oxford University Press.

Gupta, S.L. 1978. *Pandit Madan Mohan Malaviya: A Socio-Political Study*. Allahabad: Chugh Publications.

Hoare, Q. and G.N. Smith (ed. and trans.). 1992. *Selections from the Prison Notebooks of Antonio Gramsci*. New York: International Publishers.

Jones, K.W. 1976. *Arya Dharam: Hindu Consciousness in 19th Century Punjab*. Delhi: Manohar.

King, S.R. 1994. *One Language, Two Scripts: The Hindi Movement in Nineteenth Century North India*. Bombay: Oxford University Press.

Misra, J.P. 2016. *Madan Mohan Malaviya and the Indian Freedom Movement*. New Delhi: Oxford University Press.

Naik, J.P. and S. Nurullah. 1992. *A Students' History of Education in India*. Madras: Macmillan India Limited.

Nurullah, S. and J.P. Naik. 1943. *History of Education in India during the British Period*. Bombay, Calcutta, Madras, London: Macmillan & Co. Ltd.

Pal, B.C. *Mrs Annie Besant.* Madras: Ganesh & Co. Publishers.

Parmanand. 1985. *Mahāmanā Madan Mohan Malaviya: An Historical Biography (Vol. I).* Banaras Hindu University, Malaviya Adhyayan Sansthan.

Renold, L. 2005. *A Hindu Education: Early Years of the Banaras Hindu University.* New Delhi: Oxford University Press.

Sarkar, S. 1994. *The Swadeshi Movement in Bengal (1903–08).* New Delhi: People's Publishing House.

Sastri, S. 1911. *History of the Brahmo Samaj (Vol. I).* Calcutta: Published by R. Chatterji.

Singh, S. 2022. *Educational Philosophy of Madana Mohan Malaviya.* New Delhi: Atlantic Publishers & Distributors.

Sweezy, P.M. 2016. *The Theory of Capitalist Development: Principles of Marxian Political Economy.* Delhi: Aakar Books.

Trautman, T.R. 2004. *Aryans and British India.* New Delhi: Yoda Press.

Wood, E.M. 2002. *The Origin of Capitalism: A Longer View.* London, New York: Verso.

About the Author

Saumya Dey is a professor of history at Rishihood University, Haryana. He completed his PhD from Center for Historical Studies, JNU, New Delhi. His chief research interests are cultural and intellectual history and the politics of colonial India. His prior books are *Becoming Hindus and Muslims: Reading the Cultural Encounter in Bengal, 1342–1905* (Munshiram Manoharlal, 2015), *The Cultural Landscape of Hindutva and Other Essays, Historical Legitimacy of an Idea* (Shubhi Publications, 2019 [Revised Edition, 2023]), *Narrativizing Bharatvarsa and Other Essays* (Shubhi Publications, 2021 [Revised Edition, 2022]), *The Seedbed of Pakistan: Cultural Conflicts, Elite Muslim Anxieties, and the Congress, 1885–1906* (Vitasta Publications, 2023), and *Being Hindu: A Political History from Aditya Chola to Narendra Modi* (BluOne Ink, 2024).